THE BHOKSA-A LITTLE KNOWN TRIBE OF U.P.

(A. Socio-economic study)

by

Niranjan Kumar Ghatak

R. N. BHATTACHARYA
KOLKATA 2003

Published By

R. N. BHATTACHARYA

Publishers and Booksellers (Exporters)

6, M. M. Feeder Road

P. O. : Ariadaha, Kolkata - 700 057

Phone : 564-7048, Fax : 91-33-564-7048

e-mail : rnbhatta@satyam.net.in

www.http.rnbhattacharya.com

First Edition : 2003

ISBN : ISBN 81-87661-29-1

9 788187 661290

Price : Rs. 400/- $25.00

Laser Setting by :

R. N. BHATTACHARYA

6, M. M. Feeder Road

P. O. Ariadaha

Kolkata - 700 057

Printed by

MPR PRINTERS

9A, Khetra Dhole Lane

Kolkata-700 005

FOREWORD

The Sub-mountainous region which forms a narrow belt from north to west in the Central Himalaya, has been inhabited by various ethnic groups, both tribal and non-tribal, their interesting cultural patterns and peculiar way of life evoke interest to the Anthropologists and also to others. The Bhabar and the Tarai areas of sub-mountainous region are mainly inhabited by tribal societies, like the Bhoksa and the Tharu.

The Bhoksas, are one of the five Scheduled tribes of Uttar Pradesh with a total population of 23,317 of 12,444 (53.4%) are males and 10,873 (46.6%) females. Majority of the Bhoksas (90.9%) live in rural areas while the rest live in urban areas. These people are found only in four districts of U.P. namely Nainital, Dehradun, Bijnor and Pauri-Garhwal. In the past, they were found to inhabit in the unhealthy, swampy, malarious areas of Tarai region and hence, had been part to physical and cultural isolation to some extent.

The Bhoksas are basically agriculturists. They get cash through labour, as secondary source of income. Their society is divided into a number of sub-groups which are exogamous. In this patrilineal society, inheritance, descent and succession are followed through the male line. They have their own panchayat. They follow local Hinduism and worship Hindu deities. The Bhoksa culture portrays a number of unique customs in their traditional form. With their agrarian economic base, simpler unilineal stratification, traditional political unit, unique belief system and own pantheon of deities and spirits, were subject to the influence of the external and/or internal forces. Their contact with the neighbouring caste groups, impact of modern education, new legislations and modern communication, market and cash economy etc. have brought about a gradual change in their culture. These have drifted them from their traditional pattern of culture to a great extent and have given them a new entity.

Considering these features it has been proposed to undertake an intensive study among these people, living in two different areas, Nainital and Dehradun.

The present research work is thus based on following aspects :-

(1) Ecological adaptation.

(2) Economic organisation and changes in their society.

(3) The nature of sub-groups and its functioning in macro and micro levels within a particular ecological set up.

(4) To study the network of relationship within the sub-groups and community.

(5) The structure of their political system and village council.

(6) Magico-religious beliefs and practices.

(7) To identify the nature and extent of change in their society due to various factors.

Although the tribe and its cultural tradition are quite interesting yet no in depth study has so far been done on this tribe, particularly those living in Dehradun and Nainital districts. The main objective behind the present research work is to fill up the existing gap a knowledge on the Bhoksa tribe. This study would reveal how the Bhoksas have developed their existing socio-economic condition and maintained a distinct life style in a particular ecological set up and also to ascertain the nature and extent of changes in their socio-economic life and the factors responsible for these.

Two villages from each district have been selected for the study. After comparison the variation of culture between these two groups, is expected to be revealed. All anthropological methods like genealogical, case-history, interview or other methods have been applied to study this group living in two different areas.

P. K. Bhowmick

ACKNOWLEDGEMENTS

I feel much honoured in tendering my deep debt of gratitude to the Director General/Director, Anthropological Survey of India for allowing me to work in the projects. (i) Ethnographic study and Culture changes (ii) Customary laws & (iii) Education among the Bhoksas of U.P.

I also take this opportunity to show my deep gratitude to Dr. M. K. Raha, of Anthropological Survey of India for discussion related to different aspects of projects and valuable suggestion in conducting the field work.

I owe a great deal to Prof. P. K. Bhowmick for my earlier training in Anthropological theory and field-research. I take this opportunity to show gratitude to my respected teacher. Prof. P. K. Bhowmick of Calcutta University for his inspiring guidance, and keen interest in my research work.

Thanks are also extended to Mrs. M. Hazra, Mr. J. Chakraborty, Mr. & Mrs. Nanda, Mr. M. Haque etc. and other office colleagues of Anthropological Survey of India for their catholic co-operation. I also want to express my gratitude to secretary, P.K. Devad, of Servants of India Society, Bajpur for extending help and co-operation in conducting field work. Last but not least

Mr. R. N. Bhattacharya of R. N. Bhattacharya publishers and bookseller initiating the work and complete with save in book form within a short period in time.

I will be failing in my duty if I do not express my gratitude to my Bhoksa friends who provided all possible assistance in collecting data. Among them Khum Sing, (Khumbari village) Bachu Sing, Prem Sing etc. disire special mention.

Niranjan Kumar Ghatak

CONTENTS

TABLE

Chapter - One

INTRODUCTION

I

The Bhoksas are one of the five Scheduled Tribes of Uttar Pradesh. They have acquired the said status since 1967 (vide the Constitution Scheduled Tribes, Uttar Pradesh order, 1967). Before 1967, the Bhoksa or Buksa were treated in the category of Scheduled Caste in Uttar Pradesh. But the community was deleted from the list of Scheduled Caste in 1956 and again placed under the category of 'Other Backward Classes'. The Backward Classes Commission (1954) has, however, earlier recommended for the inclusion of Bhoksa or Buksa in the list of Scheduled Castes. It may be mentioned here that till 1967 no community was notified as a Scheduled Tribe in Uttar Pradesh. However, many competent observers were in favour of inclusion of the Bhoksa or Buksa in the list of Tribes. According to 1971 census, the total Bhoksa population in Uttar Pradesh is 23,316 persons, forming 11,74% of the total Scheduled Tribes population of the State, of which 90.64% live in the village areas and the rest inhabit urban and semi-urban centres. The Bhoksas are mainly found in four districts of Uttar Pradesh, viz., Nainital, Dehradun, Bijnor and Garhwal.

The district wise break up of the population of the Bhoksas or Buksas as returned in the different Censuses has furnished in table 1:1.

TABLE : 1: 1

Distribution of the people (Census Years) :

District	1881	1891	1901	1911	1921	1931	1941	1951	1961	1971
Bijnor	—	—	288	—	1177	304	202	—	783	3173
Garhwal	—	—	256	518	7	631	47	—	633	409
Nainital	—	1208	4364	5974	6285	6683	—		9330	12910
Faizabad	—	—	—	—	3	—	—	—	—	—
Sultanpur	—	—		—	18	—	—	—	—	—
Benaras state	—	—	—	—	120	—	—	—	—	—
Dehra Dun		—	—	145	—	—	—	—	—	5589
Bulandsahar	—	—	16	—	—	—	—	—	—	—
Agra	—	—	—	—	—	—	25	—	—	—
	5664	1208	4924	6637	7610	7618	274	—	10,746	22,081

Estimated.

District-wise break up is not available.

From table 1:1 it is clear that Nainital district has remained the most important area of concentration of the Bhoksas, except during 1941 census. The other two areas, which have shown some concentration of the Bhoksa, with a degree of consistency are Garhwal and Bijnor. The erratic changes registered during the different census, seem to reflect more the accuracies of enumeration, than any actual change of population. The number of Bhoksas returned from other areas, during some of the censuses has perhaps represented only temporary migrants, because they are not known to have permanent settlements in those areas.

TABLE 1:2

Yearwise Concentration of Bhoksa Population

Census Year	Population	Variation
1881	5,664	—
1891	1,208	- 4,456
1901	4,924	+ 3,716
1911	6,637	+ 1713
1921	7,610	-+ 973
1931	7,618	+ 8
1941	274	- 7,344
1961	10,746	+ 10,472
1971	22,081	+ 11,335

II

There is no detailed and complete study about the physical characteristics of the Bhoksas. Little attention has been given to this community since 1865, as Dr. J. L. Steward has made some somatoscopic observations on the Buksas of Bijnor district and described them as..

> The members of the tribe are short statured and very sparse in habit in both respects, some somewhat exceeding the ordinary Hindu peasants of the district, from whom they do not differ much in general built and complexion. No measurements of their crania were made, but so far as ordinary inspection goes their features are marked by several of the Turanian peculiarities. Thus, the eyes are small the opening of the eye-lits being narrow, linear and horizontal. (The inner angle not inclined downwards so far as I observed). The face is very broad across the cheek-bones and the nose is depressed, thus increasing the apparent flatness of the face, the jaw is prognathous and the lower lip thick, and the moustaches and beard are very scanty. (Stewart, 1865, Part II; pp. 150-151).

Bhattacharya (1937) has described the physical features of the Buksas of Kashipur Pargana of Nainital district as follows :

> They are a physically well-built people having a combination of both the Rajput and the Mongoloid traits. They are of medium stature and possess skin colour varying from light brown to medium brown. Some of the Bhoksa men and women have fine leptorrhine nose, light skin colour, long medium waved hair and they have no oblique eye slits and epicanthic folds. The women are slender and graceful in youth and quite attractive in appearance. In a few cases, the Bhoksas do show the presence of Mongoloid eye-slits and folds in general. Though not as a rule, but the existence of the fine nose and normal growth of hair on body and face cannot be denied. (Bhattacharya, 1957 : Vanyajati : Vol. V : No. 4, pp. 184-85).

A study on height, vertex and somatoscopic observations of some unrelated adult male Buksas in Bazpur Tehsil of Nainital district was conducted during the Census Operation of 1961 and an observation thereof is quoted below :

> The Bhoksas are generally of medium stature, their height vertex ranges from 157.5 c.ms. to 170 c.ms., the mean being 164.5 c.ms. The tallest individual recorded in the sample was 170 cms. in height and the shortest one was 157.5 cms. The complesion of the exposed portions varies from yellow brown to medium brown, 20% having yellow brown skin colour and the remaining 80% having medium brown. The hair on their head are straight or low wavy. They usually have round faces with medium cheek-bones, in some cases, however, their cheek-bones are quite prominent. The lips are mostly medium in thickness. Slight prognathism (projection of face or jaws) is evidenced in only 15% cases, while marked prognathism is found in 7% cases, the remaining 78% do not betray any prognathism at all. Their eye-slights are mostly straight as only 15% have oblique eyes and in only 7% cases epicanthic fold is present while it is absent in the remaining 93% cases.

Mr. S.M.H. Rizvi and Mr. V. K. Tandon, in 1975 described them as follows :

> Rate of growth at a particular age level for stature, sitting height and weight were tested of about 180 male children, aged 7-18 years, from the Bazpur Tehsil of Nainital district. In this study, they have said that their : stature Mean Value gradually increases between 7 and 18 years, showing a continuous growth. The maximum rate of growth is in the age group of 9 to 10 years. The growth velocity is maximum in the age group of 8-9 years. Their sitting height also shows continuous growth from 7 to

18 years, because the mean value increases gradually. The rate of growth is maximum in the age group of 8-9 years. The growth velocity is maximum in the age group of 12 to 13 years. Regarding weight, the same pattern is also revealed as above. (Continuous growth). The rate of growth is maximum in the age group of 9 to 10 years and the growth velocity in the age group of 14-15 years

He concluded with the remarks that the mean value of the measurement shows a continuous increase from 7-18 years. But they do not exhibit any regularity in their quantum of growth with the increasing of age.

III

The term 'Bhoksa' is a controversial one. The original meaning of the word 'Bhoksa' is still unknown. A reference to the Bhoksas is found in 'Ain-I-Akbari', a chronical of historical events during Akbar's time. There is mention of the term in it as 'Bhuksar' or 'Bhoksar', a Mughal community of Tarai region during the time of the Mughal king Akbar. In it, the location of the 'Bhoksar' referred to in the chronical coincides with the present Pargana of Rudrapur in Bazpur Tehsil of Nainital district, which is even now an area of fairly high concentration of the Bhuksar. In fact, at Rudrapur still there exists a dense forest which the local call 'Bhuksar', a jungle which is full of wild animals. According to the Bhoksas themselves, they were the denizens of the area in the forest. So, the term 'Bhoksa' may have been derived from the place name of their original habitats, in the past.

Some Bhoksas are of opinion that the name 'Bhoksa' was given to them by outsiders, as they lived in dense forest and maintained a position of complete isolation from the other people living nearby and they were in the habit of taking meat of wild animals, forest roots, i.e. 'burga' eating spoit rice (Busha-hua-khana) and dried flesh of wild animals. For all this, they earned the name of 'Bhoksa', implying eaters of every kind of food. Thus, the term was given to them by reffering to their food-habits and living conditions in the forest. Mr. Crooke (1896 : 56) has written :

> The Bhoksas are an isolated tribe. They have acquired a reputation for sorcery and witchcraft. In fact, the 'Bhoksa' is a name for a sorceror in Garhwal district.

The outsiders, however, hold another view. They think that 'Bhabar' and 'Tarai' region was an infamous malaria-ridden area. The people who were unable to tolerate the dangerous attack of 'Malaria Bukhar' or malaria fever were termed as 'Bhoksa'. But the Dehradun Bhoksas identified themselves as Mehra. Their version about the meaning and origin of the term Mehra is that the term 'Bhoksa' means a group of men who are still in the forest. They love forest and know the ins and outs of it. They refer to an anecdote in support of their statement. The story runs as follows : A British hunter came to the forest of the Siwalik Hill and lost his way. He was escorted back to his camp by some of the Bhoksa ancestors. The hunter in question, after being rescued, started addressing them as 'Mehra' i.e. a group of men who have skill in forest. Consequent upon this incident, they assumed the name 'Mehra', as derived from the event. This story has been supported by Amir Hasan. He has written :

> A British officer, who on being lost in the forest was escorted back to camp safely by a Bhoksa group. (1972 : p.8).

The Bhoksas are an immigrant group. They cannot give their exact period of migration from their original habitat. They know only this much that "they have been in this part of the country at least for the last 1200 to 1400 years." (Turner : 1931 : 585). However, Crooke reports

> .... they came from the Dakkin, others from Delhi : they were expelled from Dakkin by the Marathas. The Mehra, a Dehra Dun branch say that they came into this district beyond the Ganga at the invitation of Raja Suk-Deb-Sha of Tehri, who used them as guides through the jungles on his shooting expeditions. (Crooks : 1896 : 56).

They fix this migration into Dehra Dun at some five or six generations from the Present day (ibid).

According to Elliot :

> The Bhoksas claim to be Panwar Rajputs and assert that their chief, Udaijit, was driven away from his home after a quarrel with his brother Jagat Rao, the Raja of Bharanagar and came to dwell with a few followers in 'Banabash' (exile) on the banks of the Sarda river. Udaijit had not been there for long, when his aid was solicited by the Raja of Kumaon whose territories required defence against some of the neighbouring powers. The efforts of Panwars succeded in defending the territories of the Raja whose gratitude induced him to offer his territories. They there upon left this 'Banabasha' and came to stay in their personal abode. (Ibid. Crooke 1896:56).

The Bhoksas of both the districts, viz., Nainital and Dehradun have told many stories to justify their migration, all those stories reveal more or less the same facts that they migrated from their original habitat due to fear of Muslim worriors, who battled afterwards and committed every kind of devastation and revenge on the people of the land.

IV

The origin and the base of the community is very difficult to trace. But, according to Blunt (1931), 'There are two accounts of their origin - one is a comparatively simple story which fixes them as Rajputs from Delhi, who were voluntarily here or were exiled to the Tarai, during the Mughal period. The other story afloat is to the effect that certain Rajputs, being about to rebel against the Mughal ruler, sent their wives with their maidservants as an escort of Kahars to safety, through this wild track." The rebellion failed. Their husbands were all killed and the Bhoksas were supposedly the offsprings of the union of Rajput women and their Kahar servants." (Blunt, 1931:218).

The Dehra Dun Bhoksas say that after defeat of their king in a battle with a Muslim warrior, It was not possibe form them to live in their household, because their life and the chastify of the women folks were at stake. The Muslim warriors not only damaged their property, but also were eager to get the girls in their possessions. so, they fled into the jungle to save their life and chastify and also protect their community from the danger of total annihilation. They now do not remember the name of the Hindu king and the land of their original habitat. The Nainital Bhoksas also told the same story. They tell that after the death of king Jagat Deo, Daranagar was attacked by the Muslims who were once defeated by Jagat Deo with the blessings of goddess 'Chandi'. Jagat Deo had two sons- Jagga and Gulgulia. Both of them were ready for a fight, but they hesitated to do so thinking that the defeat might lead to the end of the community at the hands of the Muslims who were previously repulsed by their father. As a precautionery measure, the king ordered the women and children should be sent to a safe place in charge of their main-servants. Only the warriors should be in Daranagar for a final showdown. If they won the battle, the women and the children would be escorted to their families from the forest hideout and, if they lost, at least their sons would remain alive in the world. This was the history of their migration into Tarai.

According to some Muslim historians, however, 'from the 11th century onward, this area (Tarai and Bhabar) as well as the community have faced from time to time the Muslim invadors. But, particularly in the 13th century these tribes suffered cruelty at the hands of Nasir-Ud-din and Giyas-Ud-din Babar. Again, Feroz Sha sent an army into this area in order to mulot them of whatever they were left with and to take revenge and destroy for their audacity to face the Muslim army. They saw to it that they could not stay in the area in future.

The Bhoksas identify themselves as 'Thakur' claiming their origin in the line of Rajput descent. They are patriachal and the rules govern both inheritance of property and residence after marriage are followed by them as patrilineal. They follow patrilineal descent and patrilocal resident. Although Bhoksa society is an admixture of some social groups and these groups are also segmented into a number of sub-groups, yet their interactional pattern does not suggest any kind of social hierarchy existing among them. The sub-group names among them have perhaps been derived from their different place names of original settlement, in the remote past.

V

In this connection, it requires to be mentioned that many sub-groups do not exactly know how they have owned their sub-group nomenclature. The Bhoksas of Nainital district say that the present

Bhoksa population is an admixture of seven common caste groups, viz., Rajpur, Ahir, Bania, Dimar or Khahar, Chamar, Nai and Dhobi. These groups migrated long ago to this part of the country, either for fear of the Muslim invaders or for some other unknown reasons. In those days, these groups were living in the jungle and each of these groups had their separate identity. As they were living in dense forest, they had no opportunity for interaction with the outside world, even they had no connection among themselves. These seven groups could not meet one another due to fear thinking them to be enemies to one another.

The area was highly malarial and unhealthy. At the same time, the groups were much afraid of the existence of malevolent spirits like Okhya, Majhi etc., because these spirits, they believed, could cause death to human beings. Besides, they were afraid of ruthless Muslim invasions. Being sandwitched in between adverse conditions, all the groups began to think out a way to protect themselves. As all the groups were living in the same forest, they gradually came in contact during hunting or collecting jungle produces. In this way, the groups became familiar to one another. Then they took into their head that if they would have to live in the forest, they must be united to protect themselves from the inimical human beings, wild beasts and supernatural elements. The groups therefore decided to merge into a single community. So, they resolved that, as there are low castes like Dimar, Chamar, Dhobi etc., they would form a group at the cost of the caste distinctions and they would start living by giving up the traditional callings and should try to sustain on hunting-and-gathering, like the Rajputs. They might practise a little agriculture to augment their slender economy. Thus, they formed a new group having 'Namak Lota' (i.e. drinking water from the same vessel by each of the group representatives) with the bonds that they should follow the instructions of their community representatives, being a member of the same group or community in the forest of Bukshar, who began to refer themselves as Bhoksas. They took their clan or Khera name from their area of settlement and gave up their traditional clans.

The Pahari Bhoksas say that they came from the hill area and at first they settled in the hill tracts of Harbatpur in this district. As they lived with the hill people, they were called 'Pahari'. Though Bhoksas classify themselves into three groups, viz., Mukhaddam, Mehra and Pahari, all the groups love to be termed as 'Mehra'. The Bhoksas of Dehradun district say that their society is an admixture of some groups. They do not remember their sub-group names. At present, they classify the Bhoksa society into three groups, i.e., Makadam, Mehra and Pahari. None of these groups has any social significance. But by refering these names or group names they only give some incident of the past or place of their migration, from where they came to this area.

As the Bhoksa groups of Dehradun said, they settled in this part of forest lands and practised agriculture with the help of land Zemindar. One of these groups address themselves as Mukhardam, refering a conflict (legel fight) between this group of Bhoksa and the local Zemindar or Tamili of Dehradun at the time of British rule, regarding the ownership of lands. This Bhoksa group was organised under the guidance of Man Sing, a Bhoksa of Chambawal clan. In this legal fight, this group won the decree of the British court and got possession of the lands. So, they feel happy and glad to refer themselves to the name (Mukhardam). They said that they lived in this part or area since long past. The second group, Mehra, were fond of loving in the forest. They have the habit of collecting roots and tubers from the forest and they preferred hunting. They said that general tendency of the people of this group is to spend more time in the forest than in agricultural field. They said that there was a goddess, Sakumbura (one of the 108 forms of Chandi that found mention in the Chandi), in the deep forest on the other side of the Siwalik hills. Their traditional settlement was in that part of the area.

VI

Every Bhoksa (Khera) habitation consists of several clusters of conical huts arranged in lineal pattern (in Nainital district) in such a manner that a portion of the shed or roof of the hut is interlinked with the other huts. But, in Dehra Dun the arrangement is in a topsyturvy manner, and in sprawling areas. Sometimes, we find that the distance between one hut and another is more than even 50 yards. The arrangement of huts is invariably based on kinship basis. Close kinsmen, like brothers, brothers-in-law build their huts very close to each other. Bhoksa settlement, in general, is uni-ethnic. Bhoksas prefer to live in isolation among their people only, but some of the settlements have a mixed population in which other caste and community people also live along with the Bhoksas. Thus, it is very clear that the Bhoksas are gradually increasing in number and this has compelled them not only to readjust themselves with their environment, but also with the technology introduced and with the new groups of people elsewhere for their essential needs of life. In the traditional forest setting, there were some other groups who lived along with the Bhoksas. These groups were Muslims, Punjabi-Sikhs and others belonging to lower castes and also higher castes. Thus, the village inhabited by the Bhoksas may be grouped broadly into three categories, viz.,-

1. The village exclusively inhabited by the Bhoksas;
2. The village inhabited by multi-ethnic population where they are found to live not only amongst various castes, high and low, but also with the Muslims; and
3. The village where the Bhoksas live with other groups but where the Bhoksas are the dominant group.

The Bhoksa houses are generally rectangular in shape. Most of the houses consist of one bed-room and a kitchen under the same roof. The huts can be divided into three types, basing on the materials used for their construction, e.g.-

a) A pucca-house is made of burnt brick-walls with cement plaster and reinforced concerete roof ;

b) 'Chan' house is constructed of unburnt bricks, which are made by themselves, with mud-plastered walls and corrugated iron sheet or asbestos roofing.

c) The third type is the 'cutcha' house made of mud-plastered walls and thatched with 'fush', a kind of locally available grass, shade. This type of houses are very much prevalent in the village areas. The floors of the 'cutcha' house are not cemented, but the eastern floor is beaten to make it hard. The walls are made of thatching grass or reeds mixed with mud-mortar and cowdung on both the sides. The roof is not inclined too much and is covered with a grass-tatching. The branches of trees and timbers are used for construction of the frames on which the roof rests. These articles are also used as posts and poles in constructing the house.

The Bhoksas take the help of non-Bhoksa labour only when constructing a pucca house. But in case of Chan house or 'Cutcha' house they themselves build it up. Building is made by the contractors or a mason. It is a planned house. For construction of a house, a pandit is consulted to find out a suitable date to begin with the construction work. The local sorceror is consulted to select the place for the building and the sorceror also helps to ward off the evil influences of 'Bhutt' or any other sorts of supernatural agency. Generally, plinth is made only in the case of pucca house or Chan house. In a building, plinth is made with the instruction of the contractor or the mason. To lay the foundation, a plinth of 1' depth is dug in accordance with the plan of the building. Then this plinth is filled with stones and mud and hammered to give it consistency. Thus, the plinth of the house is completed. After completion of the plinth, the mason or contractor builds the walls and roof gradually. Chan house is made by themselves. Sometimes they hire labourers who know the work of wall making. Sun-dried bricks are used to erect a wall. Then 'Pharak' or 'Chapper' is made with the help of branches of the trees and timber. Wooden work is done by the local 'baddi' (Carpenter). The house is constructed on two central pillers on the two sides of the plinth. These pillars must be fixed at a depth of three feet in the ground and about 15 to 20 feet in height above the ground. Four posts of equal height are fixed at the four corners at equal distances from the central pillar. The thatched pillars are plastered with mud which open out on a large courtyard. The inner side of the wall of the Varandah is the wall of the living room. The walls are artfully decorated, with various drawings. Some of them resemble sketches of flower plants and some other with crude ones of animals and plants. The drawings are made by cutting the mud walls and then neatly plastering over it with cowdung paste. The cattle-shed is built at a distance from the front or backside of the house.

VII

They (the Bhoksas) keep their house and the courtyard clean and tidy, and do this job daily. Occasionally, they plaster the walls and ground of the house with clay mixture. This gives the courtyard a neat and clean look. They also clean their cattle-shed regularly and the garbages are stored in a soak-pit which is always located at a considerable distance from the main habitation. The villages of Nainital district, on the whole, are generally found neat and tidy, but those in Dehradun, though the villages try to keep them clean, yet due to the dispersed condition of the settlement and planless arrangement for storing the garbages of the houses and cattlesheds, this is not possible. Their main source of drinking water is a hand-pump. The Bhoksas dig small pits near the hand-pump to store water. Through canals and ditches, they allow surplus water to flow out of the pits. This precaution is taken to avoid stagnation of waste-water. As the area is highly malarious, the villagers have learnt to be careful about their natural enviornment. The Bhoksas take care in the matter of their personal hygiene. They take bath regularly and wash their clothes, when needed. But the poor Bhoksas of Dehradun district are not able to maintain cleanliness, like others, and take adequate steps about hygiene and personal physical care.

VIII

The Bhoksas are non-vegetarian and they take mutton, pork, fish and egg. Their staple food is rice with 'dal' (pulse). Generally, the Bhoksas eat what they grow. In the past, they were growing only paddy and many varieties of pulses, but at present they produce a wide variety of food grains. So, their food is enriched by a number of items of their own field products. Now they not only eat rice but also take wheat, maize etc. along with it. They take only two square meals a day - once in the morning, around 10 or 11, and again in the evening, i.e., between 4 and 6 P. M. They drink tea in the morning and also at noon or some-time in the afternoon. As has been mentioned earlier, the Bhoksas are non-vegetarian and they prefer fish to eat. Generally, their women catch fish from the canals, streams and rivers, if not regularly, but frequently. Their male folks also take part in the fish catching operations, if fish is plenty at any place. They also take meat of goat, chital, hen etc., but beef eating is a taboo to them. They do not however take meat of the dead animals. They take milk regularly and also fruits, whenever available. But about fruit eating, they occasionally are compelled to take it for their health, if doctors advise, or on some special occasions. Smoking is a fairly common thing among both men and women Bhoksas, sitting together. Hookka or the traditional hubble-bubble is their oldest smoking medium. They only allow their hookas to be smoked on to their community members. 'Bidi' (country-made cigeratte) is used frequently by the members of the community as also by the outsiders. Offering a 'Bidi' is considered as a general courtesy in the society. Drinking is a very common habit among them. Both men and women are used to drinking liquor. In the past, they used to brew drinks in their own houses. Even today, at the time of any social gathering, like marriage ceremony, 'sagai' etc., they themselves prepare drinks and offer the same to their relatives and friends. Offering of drinks is considered as highly prestigious. Nowadays, liquor is available only in

'Theka' (Government contract shops) . During 'Holi' or 'Dewali' festivals, men, women and children take to drinking en-masse. However, there are many Bhoksas who are opposed to the habit of drinking, as they find that the habit of reckless drinking is responsible for the loss of their land to the outsiders. This movement does not seem to have made much impact on them. Chewing 'Pan' (betel-leaf) or 'Khaini' is not common among them. They take 'Pan' or 'Khaini' occasionally in company of their friends.

IX

The hair-style of the Bhoksa women deserves special mention. The hair of the Nainital Bhoksa women is typical; they tie their hair in the shape of a bulging ball at the middle of their head. The women seem to take the pains to arrange their hair in this fashion. The hairstyle suits them and they look graceful in it, especially when the head is covered with 'Orhni' (scarf). But nowadays many of the young women are discarding this style and adopting a simple type of hair dressing with 'Jura' (hair ball) at the back of the head. The Bhoksas love to decorate themselves, and their women are found of wearing ornaments, even a small girl wears a few items of ornament. Their girls are given ornaments at the time of marriage, both by parents and the in-laws. Generally, the ornaments are made of gold and silver. The Bhoksas lead a very simple life. Males generally wear a five-yard white 'Dhoti', a 'Kameez' and a white cap. They use under-garments, which are made by their local tailors out of Markin cloth, known as 'Malkhori' (dirt-eater). Old men do not use any under-garment. At present, the young generation are using pyjamas and shirts. Some of them are also wearing trousers and shirts. The female traditional dress is a kind of petti-coat and

'Anngia (blouse). But nowadays the Bhoksa women wear 'Sari'.

The Bhoksa women do not use costly ornaments in their day-to-day life. They wear the ornaments when they go to attend any social gathering, such as, 'Sagai', marriage and other social functions, i.e., at the time of worship of gods and goddesses. Poor Bhoksas also use ornaments of gold or rolled-gold for this purpose. The male Bhoksas generally do not wear any ornament, but in some special cases, some of them use 'Kundal' (ear-rings) on their ear or ears. Use of 'Kundal' for the male is generally instructed by the local 'Bharara'. If the children of the family die frequently, then the 'Bharara' advises the father to make the new born male child to wear a 'Kundal'.

Tatooing, i.e., 'Godna' is found prevalent among the Bhoksas. It is frequently found among the women, some men also do the tattooing, specially their names on the forearms. Some of the women make 'Gundi' marks on their forehead by tattooing. Though tattooing is found prevalent yet it has not been given social importance and gradually it is going to fade out.

In the traditional forest setting, some other groups are found to live along with the Bhoksas. These are : Muslims, Punjabi-Sikhs and some other communities belonging to lower castes or high castes. It has been observed that in spite of intermingling with the other groups of people, the Bhoksas have a preference to living in segregation, either in jungle or in the fringe areas of the multi-ethnic villages. But, in general, the Bhoksas are found to live in uni-ethnic villages. This segregation state however does not prevent them from interacting, specially on economic ground. In some villages, the researcher found the caste groups, like Baniya, Gujar, Rawat, who are land holding groups, living side by side with Nai, Badai, Lohar, Muslim and so on. This wider social environment, in course of time, extended social relations, sometimes accentuating the process by accepting food, or rejecting it, which establishes a higher social position in the regional ethnic setting. As the Bhoksas claim to be of Rajpur status, considering themselves as the descendants of king Jagadeo of Dharanagu, the lower caste people, such as, Nai, Bhayi, Moochi etc. accept food from the hands of the Bhoksa. But the Bhoksa do not accept food, nor even water from their hand. Similarly, the other high caste groups, such as, Baniya, Rajput etc. do not even accept water from the hand of the Bhoksa. Though the Muslim communities have no such caste prejudice, it is also found the Muslim communities do not also, on occasions, accept food from the hands of the Bhoksas considering them inferior to the Muslims in status. Of course, there are local variations and in many cases the earlier views are changing rapidly.

Chapter - Two

THE SETTING

I

The tribal people are generally considered to be autochthonese and as such, they have to live close to nature. Naturally, therefore, their cultural behaviour or traits, in many cases, have sprung from the interaction with nature. Gradual give-and-take with other groups of seemingly advanced people pushed them to the unhealthy, rugged and undulating forest clad terrains, which are sometimes criss-crossed with broad, turbalant and gurgling streams that diminished the possibility of their interaction with the other ethnic groups and sealed them off into a forced ecological isolation, making them entirely dependent on nature. This forced dependence, with their crude technological adaptations, since the incomprehensibly hoary past, fostered in them a type of 'primitivism' which is betrayed in their culture.

The sub-mountainous region of the Central Himalayas comprising the 'Bhabar' - a narrow strip lying immediately below the foot-hills, and the Tarai - is a deep and marshy tract. In fact, xxxxxxxx

The sub-mountain region of Uttar Pradesh is a narrow belt from Gorakhpur, on the easternmost districts of U.P. to western-most district of Dehradun and adjoining Himachal pradesh and bounded in

North by Nepal and Almorah, Chamoly, Tehri and Uttarkashi districts of Uttar Pradesh. The sub-mountain region of Central Himalaya is the habitat of the Bhoksa community which comprises the Bhabar and Tarai. The Bhabar is a narrow belt between the Jumna and the Sarda and more particularly at the foot of the Kumoan Hill, usually covered with forest and remarkable for the total absence of water, a phenomenon which is entirely characteristic of this tract. This belt of waterless forest-land is called the Bhabar or 'Ukhar Bhumi' (waterless forest), under Kumaon and has a breadth of five to fifteen miles. Though no streams or spring exist, the Bhabar is clothed with a mangificent forest finding its nourishment in the new feet of alluvial matter that rests on the boulder and single deposit below. The Bhabar has comparatively new alluvial deposit on the inner surface of rock, boulder and gravel. The Tarai stretches from the Sarda river on the east to the Bazpur Pargana on the west, and lies between 28 43' and 29 26' north latitude and between 78 53' and 80 east longitude. It is bounded on the north by the Kumaon district, on the south, by the districts of Barelly, Moradabad, Rampur and Pillibhit, on the west by Kashipur Teshil and on the east by Nepal. The Tarai is a vast alluvial land lying at the foot of the Himalaya, bordering densely populated Gangetic plain of the south. It comprises a long narrow strip of the country running for 90 miles along the foot hills with an area of 589,359 acres or 920.8 square miles. The Tarai extends to the whole sub-mountain region, and in U.P. to the border districts of Nainital Gonda, Khiri, Gorakhpur, Pillibhit and Basti. Kashipur pargana can be best described as the meeting point of the Tarai and the plain of Rohilkhand.

The soil of the Tarai is, almost everywhere, a moist alluvial deposit. It is chiefly loam, clary and clay-sand, but the clay predominates. The soil is naturally fertile and owing to its inherent capacity, the outturn is satisfactory, so that it neither requires hard labour nor much manure on the part of the farmer. The accumulated deposit of centuries of grass and foliage has contributed to enrich the humus content of the soil with a heavy loam.

The Tarai consists of the streams and rivers which flow directly from the Himalayas and are fed by the springs originating from the swamps of the region itself. Hence, one comes across a network of springfed streams and rivers from the north to the south. So numerous are these rivers and of such little importance for the purpose that it requires scientific arrangement for irrigation. Here, an important river is Sarada. All these rivers resemble each other in their main characteristics and form the tributaries of the Ramaganga river, which falls into the Ganges in Hardoi district. As Hutton observes.

> These Tarai streams are blocked in the courses with fallen trees and overhanging branches to an extent inconceivable to one, not acquainted with them, and in high flood. The velocity is greatly diminish by their presence.

The drainage system of this tract, on the whole, ultimately leads to water logging, resulting in the creation of a happy breeding ground of mosquitoes, and finally into an unhealthy climate, as most of the rivers are susceptible to heavy floods during the rains. The proximity of the hills to the Tarai retards the proper circulation of air and makes the climate of the region very trying at all times of the year. The direct and refracted sun's heat makes it close, hot and nudgy. In general, the Tarai experiences an extreme climate, summer being severely hot and winter very cold. It receives most of its rain in june, July, August and September. Winter has only a few showers. The average annual rainfall of this region is 50 to 60 inches. During the rainy season, when the forest undergrowth grows up, climate, though enervating, is not so unhealthy. The forests of the Tarai are generally of poor value and mostly contain scrub jungles. Over a large part of the area there are a few valuable forests, except those of Traldu, Dhak, Shisham, Khai, Rauni and other Kukat trees of inferior quality; but the tract is of considerable importance as a grazing land and for fuel and fodder reserves. The presence of these forest areas has been slowly but surely encroached upon; the cultivated areas, affording wild animals greater shelter and bringing them nearer to cultivation and habitation.

These forests abound in carnivorous animals. Wild beasts, including tigers, Panthers, elephants, bears, blue bulls and many species of deer have played a lively part in the continual deterioration and destruction of the tract. The greatest amount of destruction has been done by the elephants to the villages and fields that border the forests mainly lying to the north. About a century back, tigers were numerous in these forests, but owing to the extension and growth of cultivation in recent years and also greater use of the arms and effective weapons, their number has now diminished remarkably. The panther, a kind of leopard, is much more common in this region. The four-horned antelope, a *Chasinga* (Teracers Quoricoromis), the *Jarau* (Rusa Aristotelis), *Chital* (Axix Anaculatus), *Parha,* a hog deer (Hyelapna Porcinus), are abundantly found in the grassy swamps and jungles. The wolves and jackels inhabit the whole sub-mountain region of the Tarai. Monkeys from all over Uttar Pradesh are captured and let loose in this area, as if, to play havoc with crops in the fields. Python is frequently seen in the Tarai swamps. This tract is a happy hunting ground for the ornitholo-gists, as hundreds of thousands of species of game birds, namely, jungle fowls, quails, partridges, peacocks and snipes are found in legion in the Tarai forests. In addition, fishes of all kinds and descriptions abound in the streams and rivers.

II

Kashipur Pargana of Nainital district is bounded on the north by the Kumaon Bhabar and Bijnor district on the south by Moradabad district and the Rampur State, on the east by Pargana Bazpur of the Tarai district and the Rampura State, and on the west by Bijnor district. There are only two Parganas, viz., Kashipur and Jashpur in this area. Upto 1849, Kashipur and Jashpur were two separate revenue divisions with the District Settlements and formed parts of Moradabad district. On the 1st May, 1844 the revenue division of Moradabad district was re-arranged as Bazpur, Kashipur and Jashpur along with sundry villages and formed Thakurdwara, Barkara, Moradabad and Alzemgarh which were constituted into one Pargana under the name of Kashipur. Shortly before the Mutiny, Bazpur was transferred to the Tarai, then a part of the Kumaon division. In 1960, a number of other villages were transferred to the Tarai, then in the Kumaon division, and in the same year the Tehsil of Kashipur and Thakurdwara also. In October, 1970 the entire Pargana of Kashipur was restored to the Tarai. The British Government having felt that the Kumaon division had grown unweildy for administration, created the district of Nainital, which also included the Tarai. The district in its present form came into existence on October 15, 1991. This Pargana is singularly sensitive to the variations of seasons and the climate here is varying and not uniform, even throughout the Pargana itself. Visitations of malarial fever is a hardy annual here with the exceptional changes of climate in various seasons, which is induced by the altered amount and quality of food available. With these drawbacks, the peasantry are not flourishing as one would except them, but special care is now being taken to remove the causes of unhealthy conditions which will, it is hoped, improve their present state of health and hygiene, in good time.

The Bazpur Tahsil is situated in the south-western portion of the Nainital district, having Tahsil Haldwani in the north-east, Kashipur Block in the west, Tahsil Kitcha in the east and district Rampura in the south. The Bazpur Development Block forms a part of Kashipur Subdivision. The Bazpur town is located some 110 km. to the south-west of Nainital district and 45 km. to the north-east of Rampura. It lies in the heart of the Tarai at a height of only 350 ft. above the sea-level. It is well connected with the other parts of the country. It falls onMoradabad-Lalkua section of the North Eastern Railways.

The Ramnagar Block Tahsil came into existence on the 2nd of October 1961. Its headquarters is connected by bus and Railways and its distance from Nainital is 65 km. as the crow flies. The major portion of the Block Tahsil is covered by forest. Its total area is 99.787 hectars of which 14,000 hectars, i.e., 14.5% is available for cultivation. Irrigation is available to 11.186 hectares, which works out at 80% of the total cultivable area. Motorable all-weather roads cover a distance of 64 km. The fair-weather roads are katchha and these come under the jurisdiction of the Forest Department, which covers a distance of 58 km. Katchha road linking the villages with the main roads which are in a bad shape. During the rainy season, some areas of the Block remain out off from the outside world due to spate in the rivers. During this period, one has to negotiate the area on foot. Ramnagar is a Mundi, which has links with all other roads around and is at an average distance of about 20 miles from them.

Tahsil Dehradun covers an area of 2,000.9 sq. km. This Tahsil is a succession of mountains and the gorges. The mountains are very rough with step-slopes ending in a dark chasm. These sides are sometimes wooded, but are often bare and rocky, covered at places with the hill region of Pauri Garhwal and Chamoli Tahsil in Almora district.

The Dehra sub-mountain area in the famous Dun, known as the garden of the United Provinces, lies between the Siwalik hills and the Himalayas and forms a part of the lower slopes of both. The term 'Himalaya' is properly applied only to the highest range covered with the unending snow, while the native historians always use the word 'Siwalik' to designate the outer the lower ranges of the Himalayas as well the distinct chain to which modern custom has limited to use the name. The word 'Siwalik' was formerly explained as being equivalent to 'Swawa-lakh', i.e., within the range of 1,25,000 peaks. But it is now recognised as a derivative from the name of Lord Siva. Similarly, parts of the Dun are said to be in the region particularly sacred for the god and is known from the famous temple at Kedarnath, as the 'Kedarkhand'. Along a part of their length, the Himalayas run parallel to a few miles in the south by the remnants of the ancient Siwalik range. Between these ranges lie narrow valleys, such as, the Dehradun, which border the Himalayan foothills for about 45 miles and separate the Gangetic plains from the low but rugged Siwalik hills. Here, as is the popular usage of the area, "the valley" is referred to as the Dehradun valley. The valley is about 2000 ft. above the sea level, while the Gangetic plain beyond the Siwalik is not over 1,000 ft. in elevation. It is the latter plain that is termed here as the plain, in accordance with the use by the local people. The Siwalik hills extend along the entire southern border of the Dun from the Jamuna to the Ganga, running parallel with the Himalayas at an average distance of about 20 miles. The most important feature of this tract is the ridge which separates the drainage area of Tona on the west from that of the Yamuna in the east.

The Siwaliks lie at the feet of the outer scrap of the Himalayas which bind it on the north and the sacred Ganga and the Yamuna skirt it on the east and the west, respectively. The Siwaliks on the south stop the detains flowing down with numerous mountain torrents which result in the formation of a considerably raised valley above the level of the plains to the further south. Tahsil Dehradun is densely populated (181 persons per sq. km. or 469 per sq. mile). The density of population in the rural areas of the district is 101 persons per sq. km., while in the urban area it is higher. In Tahsil Dehradun it is 1,287 persons per sq. km. The climate of Dehradun may be termed as Dr. Malaran writes:

.... a moist and temperate one. The average rainfall is 78 inches. The temperature fluctuates a shade from 17 in January to 98 in June. The month of September and October are the most unhealthy season of the year. The valley on the whole is peculiarly set, from sudden extreme heat to cold, especially from the blasts that scorch the country lying below its southern boundary, but owing to the cutting clearing and cultivating operations, which have within the last few years been carried on in the western portion of the Dun, hot winds now accompany the advent of the summer months.

These are not according to the effects, but are annually becoming more marked and prolonged, and are doubtless owing to the rapid clearance of free jungles which the land-owners think fit to carry out for cultivation. The warm breezes were known in Dehra before 1973. Due to the close proximity of the outer Himalayan Range, Dehra is also generally cold. The cold weather commences here earlier and lasts longer than it does in the plains. There are no special prevailing winds, a mild breeze blows in the warmer months during the day time wafting from the south, which changes its direction from the north after sunset. Thus, it renders the climate in the sultry season tolerable and pleasant. During the rainy season specially, its quality is so bad that it is totally unfit to live in. In fact, it is very injurious, as is noticed by the general prevalence of it at that season which leads to bowel-complaints that constitute the chief among the local ailments.

The fauna variety are many and they include deer, goats, pigs, monkeys, oxen, jackles, porcupines, bears, leopards and occasional appearances of tigers. A wide variety of birds are to be found here, including the native wild chickens. The greater part of the Dun was covered by the forests. But last year much of the forests disappeared due to marathon axing. A certain portion of the cleared land has been annexed to the villages and much of it has been invaded by tall coarse grass which is useless to both man and beast.

III

At present, the Bhoksas are settled agriculturists, But, traditionally, they were slash and burn cultivators and gatherers. Their economy has developed in very unfavourable conditions. For this, on the one hand, the Muslim invadors were responsible and, on the other, the stagnant condition of agricultural pursuits were also responsible. The ecology of the lands and their unhygienic habitations in uncongenial region are perhaps the most important factors that stood in their way to development.

History reveals that from the 11th century to the middle of the 16th, this area and its people had a traumatic experience from time to time at the hands of the Muslim invadors. From the 13th century to the middle of the 16th, the people of the area were forced to migrate from this region due to the revengeful attitudes of the foreigners to the land. According to the Muslim historian, the traditional economy of the plain tribes was interspersed with patches of grazing and cultivation. The people were chiefly occupied with pasturing cattle, scant cultivation of barley which were considered sufficient for their needs. But cultivation was influenced by the depradations of the Muslim invadors.

Muslim invadors came into the country of forest and brought much of it under the plough. (Atkinson, 1886).

Chapter - Three

VILLAGES & DEMOGRAPHIC ASPECTS

I

The Bhoksas generally live in small settlements. A traditional Bhoksa settlement used to be called *Bhusari Khera* and the name of the particular 'Bhusari Khera' was given after the name of the place or area of a person or after the name of a tree. Among the Bhoksas of Nainital district the Kheras are sometimes related to the clan or 'gotra' as the Khera i.e., the place of original inhabitation of a group, who are considered unilateral descendants of the group. There is some other economic reason for importance of a Khera in the life of the Bhoksas. It is believed that in the past, the Bhoksas used to roam about in the forest in search of food. They moved in different areas in quest of new patches of land for their shifting cultivation. But for the renewal of their old lands or to acquire some new patches, they have had to refer to the name of their old settlement to the khum authorities for their recognition as a settler of the area. Without any particular reference which is in the records of the Khum authorities, none could be allowed to renew or resettle their old lands, or permitted to cultivate some new patches of land. Most of the traditional Bhukhari Khera are the present villages of the Bhoksas, though in some cases they have adopted

Table 3:1

Particulars of the villages surveyed

Villages	Households	Population		
NAINITAL		M	F	T
1. Beria	32	107	79	186
2. Birpur	9	27	23	50
3. Pipal Sanna	30	105	113	218
4. Rajpur	24	96	93	189
5. Thari	36	102	102	204
6. Bhuri	44	197	180	377
7. Khumbari	57	180	179	359
8. Sinhali	28	86	83	169
9. Vikampuri	19	58	57	115
DEHRADUN				
10. Tiparpur	158	506	402	908
11. Midnapur & Badripur	40	130	102	232
12. Mehuwala Khalsa	43	109	101	210
	520	1703	1514	3217

some new settlements. Table 3.1 will show the particulars of the villages surveyed.

Table 3.1 depicts details of the villages surveyed along with their population structure (Bhoksa) in which males and females have been distributed on an age-group basis. In the Nainital district, nine settlement camps have been set up among which Khum Bari and the people of village Sanna are multi-ethnic groups. These are developed villages in comparison with the other roadside villages. Though the villages of these areas are near the forest enclaves, yet the above two villages have been getting more exposures to the outsiders than others, i.e., villages Beria, Birpur, Thari, Bhuri, Sinhali, Vikampuri etc.

Three villages have been selected from Dehradun district for study. All these villages are multi-ethnic in nature and are located near the forest area. The people of both the villages are settled agriculturists, where the Bhoksas also have taken to agriculture as their primary occupation. These settlements have been selected at random and the total number of Bhoksa households covered in the study are 520 consisting of a population of 3,217 of which 1,703 are males and 1,514 are females. The villages have no definite lay out plan, whether they be of a mixed population or are inhabited exclusively by the Bhoksas. It is rarely found that non-Bhoksa families are living in the midst of the settlement of other groups. The Bhoksa settlement is generally based near the forest, having an approachable cutcha road towards the villages. The main source of their water supply these days is usually the tube-wells. In addition to tubewell, there may be natural springs or rivers around the villages. In every Bhoksa village, it is observed that their tribal deity 'Bhum Sen', is represented by the elevation of a mud-mound, which is situated in front of "Podhan" (traditional head of the village) house. And the *Chomtra Than*, the place of a goddess is generally situated near a stream, and also under a big tree in the vicinity of the village.

Thus, the villages (Khera) inhabited by the Bhoksas may be grouped broadly into three categories, as follows :

1. Village exclusively inhabited by the Bhoksas ;

2. Villages inhabited by multi-ethnic population where they were found to live not only amongst various castes, high or low, but also with the Muslims and

3. Villages where Bhoksas live with other groups, but the Bhoksas are the predominant group of the village.

III

Beria, a Bhoksa inhabited village in Nainital district, falls under Block and Tahsil of Ramnagar and is situated at a distance of 28 km. and is about 20 km. from the Pargana town of Kashipur. It is a uniethnic village, only the Bhoksas live here. There are 32 households with a population of 186 persons, including 107 males and 79 females. It is the oldest village of this area and also is placed comparatively in the interior, and also situated just near the forest limits. There is no school in this village. Village Birpur is also a uni-ethnic village, only the Bhoksas inhabit there. It is the neighbouring village of Beria, though situated about 1/2 km. from the latter and 1/4 km. from Thari village. The village has only 9 households, having a total population of 50, of which 27 are males and 23 are females. Village Piplasanna lies at a distance of 23 km. and 18 km. from Ramanagar Tahsil and the Block headquarters, respectively as also at the same distance from the Kashipur Pargana town. This village is situated near the main road. It is a multi-ethnic village and some other communities, such as, Pahari Rajput, Baniya, Sikhs etc. also live here side by side. But in comparison to the Bhoksas their number is uterly insignificant. This village offers the winter residence to some hill families from time immemorial. There is a Primary School in the village. It consists of 30 households of the Bhoksas in the village with 218 members of whom 105 are males and 113 are females. Village Thari lies next to village Pipalsanna. This village is also having a Primary School. It is an uni-ethnic village, having 36 Bhoksa households with a population of 204 members, of whom 102 are males and 102 are females. Likewise, village Rajpur is also a uni-ethnic village, consisting of 24 households comprising 189 persons, of whom 96 are males and 93 are females. There is no school in this village. The students of the village go either to Pipal Sanna or Thari School for their education.

The villages of this area of Nainital district form a part of Bazpur Tahsil, and are situated at a distance of 15 km. from the Bazpur Tahsil town and 44 km. from the Pargana Kashipur town, respectively. Its head-quarters-Nainital is about 100 km. (approx.) from the village. Although most of the villages are uni-ethnic in nature, yet there are Hindu-Punjabi, Hindu-Sikhs and Mahamedans etc. living either in the proximity of the villages or there are people having one or two houses within the areas of the villages. A good number of Punjabi, Sikh and Muslim are found in the area. Village Bhuri has 44 households with 377 persons, of whom 197 are males and 180 are females. There is a Balwadi school in the village, run by the Servants of India Society, Bazpur. There is no High School in the village and the school-going children visit Banna-Khera School for their studies. The area is well connected with the Tahsil town by a metalled road. Village Khumbari is multi-ethnic in nature. This village has given shelter to Muslim and Punjabi-Sikhs along with the Bhoksas. The Bhoksas are the numerically dominant group of the village, having 57 households with a total population of 359 of whom 180 are males and 179 are females. There is a school in this village. The village is situated on the side of the metalled road which connects the Banna-Khera to Batpur-Nainital road. Village Sinhali is also a uni-ethnic one. It is situated rather in the interior and comparatively isloated from Khumbari village. It is having 28 households with 169 persons, of whom 86 are males and are 83 number of females. There is a Balwadi school in the village. The village people are also trying to run a Primary School under the supervision of the Servant of India Society. Village Khumbari is situated just after the village Vikampuri on the Banna-Khera road. A part of the village Vikampuri is on the roadside and another part is situated after a furlong off. Village Vikampuri is having 19 households with a population of 115 of whom 58 are males and 57 are females. There is no school in this village.

Village Tiparpur of Dehradun district is situated about 36 km. from the district headquarters of Dehradun. The village lies at about 5 km. from the nearest Police Station and the market town, Sahaspur. The Assam river flows in between Tiparpur village ans Sahaspur town. The village has 158 households, having 908 Bhoksa inhabitants of whom 506 are males and 402 are females. It is multi-ethnic and sprawraling in nature. Although the Bhoksas are a numerically-dominant group, the other groups, like Benia, Gujar, Harizan etc. have a good number of households here. The Gujar and the Benia are the economically dominant groups of the village. There is a Primary School functioning in the village. Similar composition is also found in Medinipur and Badripur villages. There are 40 Bhoksa households with a population of 232, of whom 130 are males and 102 are females. There is an Ashram school and also a Balwad school in this village. Mahuwala Khalsa village of Sahaspur Block of Dehradun district is situated about 26 km. from the Sahaspur

Block itself and 96 km. from the district headquarters of Deharadun. The village is having 43 households with 210 members, of whom 109 are males and 101 are females. It is a multi-ethnic village. The Bhoksas live at the outskirts of the village. Although the village forms part of the Sahaspur Block, it is the border village lying in between the Dehradun Tahsil and the Challrata Tahsil. There is a school in this village and the village comprises the Rajputs, Banias, Muslims, Harizans etc.

II

In recent times, migration to other villages has decreased, as most of the Bhoksas have become owners of landed property, in pursuance of the U.P. Tenancy Act in their permanent settlements. And thus a sense of belonging and attachment to land has developed. Since long time past, shifting cultivation was their main economic pursuit, besides the collection of forest products and, at present, they completely depend on land and agricultural activities. The forest still plays a dominant role in their life, which provides them with fuel wood, minor forest produces, especially gum and honey and sometimes even hunting small games.

Changes of settlement is generally found among the newly married couples; some of them generally prefer to live in the village of their in-laws. Sometimes, after the death of a member of the family they change their hut, if they find any symptom of existence of ghost haunting the same, especially the 'Majhi', a sort of malevolent spirit. But most frequent changes of their huts in the settlement take place when a person is in conflict with any *Bharara*, a sorceror of the community. Therefore, the owner of the hut has to leave the village of his settlement to save himself and his family from the mischief and malevolence of the 'Bharara' with their magical power. It is said, and also believed, that people die generally due to malevolence of the 'Bharara'.

III

The population structure of the Bhoksas has been reflected in table 3.2, indicating the details of age-sex distribution and many other relevant aspects of the community :

Table 3:2 reflects that out of the 3216 people studied, 1685, *i.e.*, 52.40% are males and 1,531 or 47.60% are females. The overall sex ratio is 890 females for 1000 males. This population distribution agrees with the general pattern of the country, as a whole. Secondly, age-group-wise population distribution shows that 0-14 age group persons of 1394 or 43.46% predominate the other age-group people, the population being 15-44 age group (41.09%), 45-59 age-group category 9.3% and 60 plus is 7.1% respectively. This population trend reflects the stability, *i.e.*, the working force existence of the future generation. People of age group 15-44 are quite considerable in number. The number is 1319, *i.e.*, 1319 persons is the total figure. This is believed to be the productive age group of the community, which reflects that there is considerable changes in the growth of population and the latter age groups are comparatively less. This indicates that the population is not burdended with the old and infirm generation or non-productive and non-working forces. Table 3:3 shows the marital status of the Bhoksas.

IV

The Bhoksas have been classified into four distinct groups, according to their merital status.

Table 3:2

Population Distribution by Age, Sex & Village

	Family	0-14			15-44			45-59			60-up		
		M	F	T	M	F	T	M	F	T	M	F	T
Beria	32	46	27	73	40	37	77	12	8	20	8	8	16
Birpur	9	7	10	17	15	9	24	2	2	4	3	2	5
Pipal Sanna	30	40	54	94	48	43	91	9	9	18	8	7	15
Rajpur	24	34	44	78	46	37	83	11	10	21	5	2	7
Thari	36	35	42	77	47	41	88	12	8	20	8	12	20
Bhuri	44	94	89	183	70	61	131	8	15	23	21	10	31
Khumbadi	57	73	91	164	79	71	150	12	15	27	18	4	22
Sinhali	28	48	44	92	20	36	56	6	6	12	1	8	9
Vikampuri	19	28	29	57	21	20	41	3	3	6	6	3	9
Tiparpur	158	210	174	384	208	166	374	47	36	83	41	36	77
Midnapur	40	51	43	94	59	50	109	11	9	20	5	1	6
Mehuwala	43	38	43	81	52	43	95	7	6	13	13	6	19
	520	704	690	1394	705	614	1319	140	127	267	137	99	236

T = 3216

M = 1685 (52.40%)

F = 1531 (47.60%)

These are :

1. Unmarried.
2. Married (couples),
3. Widowed, and
4. Widower,

Table 3:3 depicts the details of the marital status of the Bhoksas under study.

Out of the total of 1725 males and 1519 females, 982 males and 762 females are unmarried. The unmarried population has outnumbered the other categories, *i.e.*, both married, widows/widowers. The marriageable age of the girls has been fixed at an age between 15 and 20, or in other words, at their puberty age; and that for the boys is between 18 and 25. The number of married males is 676, *i.e.*, 39.40% and that of the spinsters is 683 or 45.02%. The married females have outnumbered their male counterparts by 7, which appears to be due to some people taking more than one wives. Generally, the first wife is taken through an elaborate marriage ceremony, whereas, the second wife is in most cases a widow or a divorced woman taken to wife. During the field survey, 67 males and 74 females were found to be widowers and widows, respectively. These persons were found to be living with their unmarried children.

The case of divorce are generally settled at the level of traditional Panchayat. Divorce is granted to a man, if the wife is barren, adulterers or in case of maladjustment. Simultaneously, an woman may seek divorce, if the husband is impotent or an adulterer, or due to maladjustment. If the wife seeks divorce, then the total expenditure of marriage incurred by her husband's family has to be returned

Table 3:3
Marital Status

Village		Married	Unmarried	Widow	Widower	T
Beria	M	46	56	—	5	107
	F	46	30	3	—	79
Birpur	M	13	30	—	1	44
	F	13	10	—		23
Pipal Sanna	M	48	50		7	105
	F	48	58	7		113
Rajpur	M	49	49		3	101
	F	44	47	2		93
Thari	M	39	53	—	10	102
	F	42	47	13	—	102
Bhuri	M	73	119	—	5	197
	F	73	100	7	—	180
Khumbadi	M	69	104	—	7	180
	F	70	105	4	—	179
Sinhali	M	30	56	—	—	86
	F	28	45	10	—	83
Vikampuri	M	21	34	—	3	58
	F	24	32	1	—	57
Tiparpur	M	189	297	—	20	506
	F	194	194	19	—	407
Midnapure & Badripur	M	52	77	—	1	130
	F	53	47	2	—	102
Mehuwala	M	47	57	—	5	109
	F	48	47	6	—	101
Total	M	676	982	—	67	1725
	F	683	762	74	—	1519
Including		1devorce				3245

to her husband. If she desires not to re-marry after divorce, but to stay with her parents, then the said amount should be paid by her father. In case she effects divorce to marry another man, then her second husband is required to pay the whole amount spent by her husband under the head of marriage expenditure. In Bhoksa society, women enjoy unique privilage in case a husband wishes to divorce his wife, but if the latter is unwilling then divorce can not be effected. Of course, if the wife is barren then he may take another wife without disolving the former marriage.

Table 3:4

Generation-wise population distribution of house hold

Village	Household	Members				Members
		First	Second	Third	Fourth	T
Beria	32	112	26	—	—	138
Birpur	9	6	—	—		6
Pipal Sanna	30	117	34	3		154
Rajpur	24	107	35	—		142
Thari	36	119	33	—	—	152
Bhuri	44	218	75	5	—	298
Khumbadi	57	199	55	14	2	270
Sinhali	28	118	10	—	—	128
Vikampuri	19	62	17	—		79
Tiparpur	158	560	134		—	694
Midnapur & Badripur	43	52	18	—		70
Mehuwala Khalsa	40	137	20		—	157
	520	1807	457	22	2	2288

As has been stated earlier, the Bhoksas are a migratory group of people. In the past, they moved from place to place in search of their livelihood. Table 3:4 reveals the facts about their settlement and population distribution generation-wise. It is evident from the said table that out of a total of 2288 persons studied of the first generation, *i.e.*, the generation of the ego, that it is 1807 persons and is predominating over the other generations, and in the second generation or the ego's parents' generation the number is 457, and in the third degree of relationship, *i.e.*, the generation of the ego's grand-father, it is only 22 and in the genration of great-grandfather it is only 2.

The Bhoksa families have been categorised, on the basis of members, as 'small', 'medium', 'large' and 'very large'. As already stated, 520 families from 12 Bhoksa villages of the two districts were studied. The families have been classified here according to their sizes.

1. Small-sized family - having 3 members or less.
2. Medium-sized family - having 4 to 6 members.
3. Large-sized family - having 7 to 9 members.
4. Very large-sized family - having 10 or more members.

Table 3:5 shows distribution of family sizes on the village basis :

Small to medium sized families are found to predominate in Dehradun district, whereas in Nainital district it shows a tendency towards medium to large families. Generally, grown up sons break away from their parents immediately after their marriage or after having a child. Then he establishes a separate family of his own, because it is very difficult to accommodate more than one family

Table 3:5

Distribution of family sizes in village basis

Village	No. of families	Family Sizes			
		Small (0-3)	Medium (4-6)	Large (7-9)	Very large (10+)
Beria	32	5	16	9	2
Birpur	9	1	5	3	—
Pipal Sanna	30	4	13	7	6
Rajpur	21	2	6	6	7
Thari	36	9	15	7	5
Bhuri	44	4	8	18	14
Khumbadi	55	9	23	16	7
Sinhali	28	4	15	6	3
Vikampuri	19	5	6	5	3
Tiparpur	148	38	73	36	1
Midnapur & Badripur	43	11	27	5	—
Mehuwala Khalsa	35	17	16	2	—

under the same roof, as the space in the house is very limited. Small-sized families are found in almost all the villages where widows and widowers live either with their minor children or alone. But of the 520 families, 109 (21.80%) have 3 members or less each. Medium sized families are predominant (numbering 223) in all the Bhoksa villages. This type of families occur in the highest percentage of 44.60%. Such a family consists of parents and their unmarried children. The number of large-sized families is 120, the percentage being 24%. In such families live parents, their married sons and unmarried children. Only 48 families (9.6%) fall under head 'very large sized' families with 10 or more members among the 520 families studied.

Table 3:6

Literacy table

District	Village	Population		0-14		15-44		45-60		61 - +	
		M	F	M	F	M	F	M	F	M	F
Nainital	Beria	46	27	—	—	8	—	—	—	—	—
	Birpur	7	10								
	Pipal Sanna	40	54			11		2			
	Rajpur	34	44	12	4	7		1			
	Thari	35	42	5		10				1	
	Bhuri	94	89								
	Khumbadi	73	91	7	1	10				1	
	Sinhali	48	44								
	Vikampuri	28	29								
Dehra dun	Tiparpur	210	174	37	2	16	2	6		1	
	Midnapur & Badripur	51	43								
	Mehuwala Khalsa	38	43								
Total		704	690	61	7	62	2	9		3	

The maximum number of members of such a family is found to be 68.

Bhoksa individuals, who are just able to read and write a little or can sign their names, are considered literates. The total numbers of the literate persons in the various age-groups in different villages covered under study is given in Table 3:6 The school-going children who have satisfied this yerdstick are also considered as literates. Out of a total population of 3217 in the 12 villages, 144 persons are considered literate. Out of these 144 literate persons, the number of literate males is 135 and that of literate females is 9. The percentage of literacy is high in the villages where exist schools in the village or any Ashram school is present in the area. In Uttar Pardesh, among the Scheduled tribes, only 22.51% of males and 5.58% of females are literates. The Bhoksa tribe possess a much less percentage of literacy, *i.e.*, 13.72% of males and 2.99% of females who are literates compared to the Scheduled tribe population of Uttar Pradesh.

V

Attendance of the Bhoksa students in the school is extremely poor, and that in the months of July and August (the agricultural season) is comparatively less than in other seasons. Bhoksas generally send their children to the school in their later age. The school has no attraction for them towards education or otherwise. As their economic condition is bad, the services of the children are essentially necessary for the family. In the matter of pursuing their studies in school, the students do not get any encouragement in their homes, which often result in the irregularity in attendance, and they feel an urge to becoming drop-outs. The Bhoksa parents do not like to send their wards far away from their village. So, non-existence of a Higher Secondary Schol and absence of proper hostel facilities, and rather non-cordial treatment, even ill-treatment from the other students of the non-Bhoksa communities, are the main causes of their desisting from going to school. Early marriage among them is also another main cause of being drop-outs.

According to the existing system, the school-going children take part actively in the execution of agricultural activities in different phases of the process. He or she is also saddled with other chores, like collection of faggots and fuel wood, tending cattle and looking after the younger children. Their services are considered inescapably necessary and are also expected of him/her being a member of the composite family. Even under such circumstances, they try to prosecute their studies. And despite all these hindrances, some of them have qualified themselves as graduates. This aspiration has been generated by the love for modern education on which they pin their faith. But the most surprising fact is that on being educated in general senses they opt out for some clerical jobs or wish to be absorbed in Banks or Railways. Thus, education in Bhoksa community is, in general, guided by the factors which are ingrained in their life-style, namely, eradication of their appaling poverty.

VI

Efforts for the educational upliftment of this tribal community was initiated by the Servants of India Society, a voluntary organisation headed by Shri P. K. Diwedi, the Organising secretary of this area. This society has opened a Boy's Hostel for the tribal students at Bazpur in Nainital district, providing free accommodation, boarding, clothing, bedding lighting, medical facilities and, on top of them all, free coaching of 63 students studying in classes VI to XII (in the Intermediate College of Bazpur). At present, the total strength of the students is 63 in the Hostel. Among them, only 13 Bhoksa students live there and the rest of the immates belong to Bhutia, Tharu and Jaunsari. The society has opened 15 Education centres throughout Bazpur Block for spreading Adult Education among the Bhoksas with the financial assistance from the Education and Social Welfare Department. The society is partly successful in their attempt. Every adult education centre has 30 adult students belonging to the age group of 15-30. some of the centres have been well accepted by the villagers, who evince sufficient interest in it. The society bears all the expenditure regarding their education. Classes of the education centres are held at night, between 7 p.m. and 9 p.m. This society has also opened 15 Balwadi schools in Bazpur area. In each of these schools there are 40 students. These are co-education schools of 2-1/2 years to 5 years. The society also provides teachers for education of the children, along with tiffin for the students who attend the school. Opinions of the students, parents and respectable gentlemen about these schools are enclosed.

Table 3:7 gives details of Non-Labour/Labour/ Working force among the Bhoksa.

The non-labour/labour/working force of the Bhoksas in the studied villages has been estimated as per census conducted by the investigates during his field-study. It is very significant that the working-force of the tribe is higher than the labour force (in 15-60 year age-group). This indicates the involvement of non-labour force in day-to-day economic activities which has been accelerated by the opportunities of employment of the Bhoksas.

Opinion about the role of Government and non-government organisation to spread education

	Government	Non-Government
1. Opinion of students.	They prefer existing education system. But not from the Government school, because it is no place for them only, it is common to all. So they feel uncomfortable in acquittance with other people.	They prefer non-government educational institutions like Borpur, Bokss boys' hostel, where somehow they feel at ease with the others and where they are provided with education and enthusiasm.
2. Opinion of parents.	Teachers do not take care of our children. Since in Government school the teachers admit students on merit basis and our children may not be able to cope with others resulting in the teachers' becoming marked on the other students.	They are of the opinion that non-government schools play important role in educating and imparting mannerism.
3. Opinion of the	Teachers do not take care of our children. Though this system is quite good to uplift the Bhoksa but Bhoksas don't feel at home with other children.	It is better to give first-hand education though the agencies of social worker so that the participation of education is with joy and fear may be dispeeled or removed.
4. Opinion of social workers	Though government system is good to them, but Bhoksa don't get benefit from this system, so they fail to keep pace with the studies of other groups.	Non-government agencies treat them more carefully, so Bhoksa feel at home with social workers. It is also better to spread their education through the Non-government agencies and that will yield the desired result.

Table 3:7
Non-Labour / Labour / Working force

Village	Population		Non-labour force				Labour force		Working force age group	
	M	F	0 - 14		61 - up		M	F	M	F
	M	F	M	F	M	F				
Beria	105	81	46	27	7	9	52	45	68	54
Birpur	27	44	7	10	3	2	17	11	22	21
Pipal Sanna	105	113	40	54	8	7	57	52	73	60
Rajpur	96	93	34	44	5	2	57	47	74	60
Thari	100	103	35	42	8	12	57	49	68	63
Bhuri	193	175	94	89	21	10	78	76	115	113
Khumbadi	180	178	73	91	18	4	89	83	93	109
Sinhali	105	77	48	44	22	1	35	32	42	39
Vikampuri	506	412	210	174	41	36	255	202	343	235
Tiparpur	36	21	12	9	3	—	21	12	30	15
Midnapur & Badripur	140	107	51	43	19	5	70	59	102	60
Mehuwala Khalsa	118	102	48	43	13	6	57	53	77	66

Chapter - Four

CHANGING ECONOMY

I

Bhoksas are now settled agriculturists. But traditionally, they were slash-and-burn cultivators, and gatherers. Their present economy has been shaped and developed in a very unfavourable situation. The major factors which were responsible for the ill-developed economy of the Bhoksas were their migratory nature (at the same time, the area and the community had suffered blows from time to time at the hands of the Muslim invadors which forced them to migrate from the region), the ecology of the land and their habitation in uncongenial region. Traditionally, they had no fixed settlement. Earlier, they wandered in the forest areas of Tarai and Bhabar as a forest dwelling community. As Mazumdar (1944) refers to them as a nomadic people moving about in search of jungles to clear for cultivation. According to some historians in the eleventh century, the area was covered with dense forest and the traditions of the plain tribes were to be interspersed with patches of grazing and cultivation of lands. The people were chiefly occupied in pasturing cattle, the scant cultivation being barely which is sufficient for their want. Their temporary dwelling places were forests to which the grazers could fly in times of danger. From the eleventh century to the thirteenth century, the Musalman invadors came into the country, and forest and cultivation were influenced by them. They brought much of the available land under the plough. But from the 13th century to the middle of the 16th century people of the area were forced to migrate from the region due to revengeful attitude of the Muslim invadors towards them. Not a single person was allowed to stay in this land and not a single acre of land was cultivated within this period. Besides this, the are is well known as a uncongenial region where heat makes it hot and sultry in the months from August to October and there prevails and extremely malarious climate and unhealthy condition for the people living in the area. The uncongenial ecological condition indirectly creates problem to them for being settlers.

During this period, their settlements were generally scattered. At that time, one hamlet was a furlong away from the other. The membership of the settlement remained a flux on accout of frequent migration of the people from one settlement to another. This migration took place for a variety or reasons, such as, search for subsistence, quarrels due to some extra-marital sex relations between a man and a woman and elopment of girls. The ties within the settlement were in feeble conditions which broke loose very easily. Close kin ties were at the best found mainly among the inmates of the hamlets. Although they practised some sort of shifting cultivation, they burn down the shurbs of the jungles and sow seeds in the ashes. The crop grown in this manner comprises Ragi or Mandua But influence of forest in the life of the community plays an important role and that still influences the life of the community members.

Economic activities of the Bhoksas were mainly based on food gathering and grazing cattle. They were heavily dependant on these. The food gathering activities were confined mainly to women and children. The gathering items were collected for domestic consumption. Though the Bhoksas had reputation of being good hunters, yet they were obliged to depend, to a great extent, on the land and on its output. The range of activities that are connected with the execution are mainly restricted to the participation of wome folks. But their instinctive love for pastoralism and gathering of food stuff from the jungle overshadowed their cultivation activities. Besides this, lack of sufficient knowledge in agriculture and attitude towards the agricultural work kept them away from the paddy field. They were also wanting to prepare good manure and to gain knowledge of irrigation. The main crops in this area are maize, barley, wheat and rice. At the time of harvesting, threshing and cleaning more hands are needed, but being a migratory group, they cannot provide it. Cultivation of more lands requires more hands and therefore they are not at ease in agricultural activities, since they are not backed up by sufficient amount of agricultural knowledge. So, marginal attention was given to agriculture, which might also be due to traditional shifting cultivation. They allow weeds and plants to grow in their field and as the sowing season approaches, they feel the growth to be useful as manures. Then they burn it, scratch the lands with a digging stick or plough and spread whatever seed they can get. Sowing of seed over a large area of land is a problem to them, because at the time of cutting, threshing and storing it requires a good number of workers.

Economic development of the area was actually started from the 16th century. In the 16th century, Tari proper was annexed with the hill state and was first to take measures to ensure the obedience of the nomads and semiburbarous inhabitants. The tract (Tarai and Bhabar) lying along the foot of the hills provides good production of yield; so, it has been growing in importance with the Kumaon rulers.

Introduction of agricultural activities into their lives might be a part of their life style, yet it is not an indispensible part, because the migratory instinct still dominate in them, So, the scope of getting them-selves equipped with a fair amount of knowledge and experience is almost limited.

II

Interpretation of individualistic approach to life is their preference to free and undisturbed way of living, even indulging in laziness and indifference to further involvement with others. This self-centered ego affects their agricultural activities for their conspicuous non-participation in the process. The Bhoksas of Dehra dun district led a nomadic life in the past. The inhabited the region of Siwalik Hill. Their present settlement is due to the influence of the Zemindar of this region. The Zemindars of this region were helpful towards the people of Bhoksa community. They promised to the Bhoksa leaders that they wished to help them in every way if they agreed to leave the Siwalik Hill area and become settled agriculturists. So, they came down from Siwalik Hills to keep their promise to the Zemindar. In the past, they were allowed to practice shifting cultivation. But gradually they became settled in this area. Later Zemindar of this area imposed on them tax of Re. 1/- to Rs. 1 and half for their lands, depending on the quality of lands for cultivation purpose. The Zemindar never allowed to cultivate the same piece of land for more than three years. Later on, the zemindar brought in people of Gujar community from the plains and settled them on the lands cleared and developed by the Bhoksas.

The Bhoksas being an agricultural community, land is of prime importance to them. For agriculture, quality of land is one of the factors which is responsible for good production of paddy. Bhoksas of Nainital district are favourably placed so far as the qualiy of land is concerned, whereas the Bhoksas of Dehra Dun district are not favourably disposed in comparison with those of Nainital. They have to struggle hard with the infertile land. The lands of the area are devided into different categories, depending on the quality of soil. These are-

(i) Bahiar - Durs - Sandy mud,
(ii) Baluar - extremely Sandy i.e. 75% sand and 25% mud.
(iii) Dumat - muddy and
(iv) Matiari - Durs mud and sand.

Out of the above, pure Matiari Durs and Dumat soils are better for agriculture. And Matiari Durs is the best quality of land for cultivation. At the same time, land is again categorised into two major groups, depending upon the availability of irrigation facilites, *i.e.*, irrigated land - 'Talati' land.... and - dry land.

III

Bhoksas use plough in their field. Some well-to-do Bhoksas have tractors. But most of them still depend on traditional bullock drawn wooden plough. A few of them also use iron plough for the purpose of cultivation.

Agricultural Implements

Name of the implements in English	Nainatal	Dehra Dun
1. Plough-made up of wooden with an iron blade	Hall	Hall
2. Yoke-made up of wood	Jot	Jula
3. Spade	Phawara	Phawara
4. Leveller	Patela	Sowga or Sawagali
5. Sickle	Hasia	Datre
6. Instrument used for plantation of paddy and removal of weeds.	Datala	Zandra
7. A small digging appliance also used as a hoe.	Dhurpi	Poula

According to agricultural calendar, particular crops are cultivated in particular months. To till the soil, they use traditional type of bullock-driven plough. Agriculture is solely a job of the males, because females are prohibited culturally to touch the plough. Both males and females work together at the time of transplantation. But females are the main labour force to work for the transplantation. Generally, males are engaged in levelling or to prepare the field for transplantation and the female transplant the seedings. Sometimes young children also come to help their parents at this time. But aged men and women do not work in the field for transplantation. They generally look after the household matters or children. Weeding are done by both males and females, sometimes children with their parents take part in this work of weeding. Threshing is done with the help of bullocks. All the family members help in storing the grain.

Table 4:1

Agricultural Calender

English Calender	Month they count	Dehra Dun	Nainital
January-February	Mag-Mah	Seeding onion, dhania, mattu, ake, tomato.	Harvesting of sugar cane and carting for crushing.
February-March	Fagun	Harvesting sugar cane, bean, mustard seeds and wheat.	Harvesting & carting of sugar cane an harvesting of wheat.
March-April	Chait	No seeding, harvesting of wheat, sericultural work.	Harvesting of wheat, carting of sugar cane, collects for basketing.
April-May	Baisak	Sericulture, ploughing the field for kharif, cutting makkai.	Ploughing the field for Kharif.
May-June	Jaith	Sericulture, ploughing the field, use manure.	Ploughing the field for makkai.
June-July	Asad	Seeding of 'dhan' seeding makkai, 'til', bajra.	Seeding of dhan, seeding makkai hoeing of sugarcane.
July-August	Srawan	Transplantation of dhan.	Transplantation of paddy, hoeing of maize.
August-September	Bado	Makkai cutting, weeding.	Weeding of plants and manuring.
September-October	Asavin	Sericulture.	Weeding of dhan.

English Calender	Month they count	Dehra Dun	Nainital
October-November	Kartic	Dhan cutting and sericulture	Rice cutting.
November-December	Mangshi	Cutting wheat.	Cutting wheat.
December	Plough	Cutting of wheat and seeding sericulture.	Cutting wheat.

At present, they use traditional manure and sometimes they also use chemical fertiliser, such as, uria, potash, sulphate, etc., for agricultural purpose. They collect these manures from the local market or from the Block office or from the cooperative society. Generally they use their traditional seeds for the sowing; at the same time, they cultivate improved variety of seeds collecting them from the respective Block Offices for their cultivation. They cultivate categories of seeds depending on the conditions of the soil. At the Kadder-where water is available, they cultivate Basmati, Ramjaonan, Darmati, Hansaraj, all of which are traditional varieties. But improved varieties of seeds, i.e., Ratna, Jaya, I.R. 420 are collected from the Block Office and on the 'Dhur' land or dry lands they cultivate Ramjaon, Newri etc. Bhoksas of Nainital district are strict to the agricultural work, whereas the Bhoksa of Dhera Dun district do other work as their subsidiary occupation. They work in the field and at the same time go on collecting fuel wood from the jungle and sell it in local market at Sashespur. Some of the Bhoksa members prepare rope which is made by twisting long grass (a kind of grass, which is available in the deep forest) and sell it in the nearest market.

IV

After establishment of the Department of Agriculture, the Bhoksa of Dehra Dun are were impressed about the efficacy of sericulture cultivation introduced by the Sericulture Office, and they have now accepted sericultural works as their secondary occupation. The sericulture gives them part-time employment. In a year, they get two change for the sericulture, in the months of March to April and again in the months of October to November. They collect the Cocoon seeds from the sericulture Department and rear these in their house. To develop a seed into a Cocoon, it takes about 45 days. During this period, the whole family members, including the children, remain busy for rearing of the same. After maturation of the Cocoon, they supply it to the Sericulture Department at a price of Rs. 18/- per kilogram.

Before independence, the area now inhabited by the Bhoksas remained comparatively isolated for the following two reasons-

(i) lac of communication e.g., in-accebility and road transport and town facilities were not there, and

(ii) the area was highly malarious.

In the past, they lived in the forest as a forest dwelling community. They made their living by food gathering, pasturing cattle and a little hunting that they could do. They were accustomed with the forest life. The forest provides them all the required materials for the settlement and supplied fruits, roots, barks etc. for their subsistence and also provides them grazing ground for their cattle or domestic animals.

V

After independence, the situation of the Bhoksa community has changed. Forest is now not free to them, as in the past when they practised sudden cultivation. Further encroachment in the forest is not possible. But due to their living in the proximity of the forest, they get some special privileges from the Forest Department. These are as follows :

1. They are allowed to collect dry wood from the forest for their personal use.
2. They are permitted to get the wooden poles from the forest, free or in the concessional

rates from the forest after having the permission of the Forest Department.

3. They are allowed to graze their domestic animals in the forest.

VI

As described by the Bhoksas, the forest is not now that rich in edible roots and fruits or other forest products as they were used to be in the past. Even then, they are the regular visitors tox the forest and also exploit the forest products for various purposes of their day-to-day life. At present, they utlise the forest for the following purposes :

(i) Collect dry wood and faggots for fuel,

(ii) Collect wooden poles for repairing old houses or for the construction of a new one,

(iii) Collect Bindgrass- a kind of grass which they use for making rope for Charpai.

(iv) Collect 'Munch' - a kind of thick grass, which is used for prepairing basket dailays, sofa, etc.,

(v) Collect 'Chalta' - a kind of herb leaves for making roofs of their houses,

(vi) Some of them are engaged to collect a kind of leaf, which is used as plates. They sell it in the local market.

Above all, forest provides ground for pasturing their cattle. Rearing of cattle is treated as a source of income to them. This is not the only consideration of keeping cattle as an unavoidable part of their plough cultivation. For plough cultivation, cattle however are required, as per their traditional custom, but they consider them as an unavoidable part of their life. On the whole, it may be said that in the past forest provided food and shelter for them. But at present, forest still supplies them with one essential material for their daily life, namely, shelter, and helps them economically by supplying forest products. Thus, forest may be treated as a source of their secondary income.

VII

The Tari are came under the British rule from the Nawab of Avuod, in 1802. Gardner was the first Commissioner of the newly acquired territory of Kumaon, including Tarai Bhabar. He was succeeded by Trail, who handed over charge to Col. Gowai, in 1831. During this period, Tarai went to Rohilkhand district. In 1839, Lushington succeeded Gowai, followed by Balten in 1848, who governed the country till 1856. During his rule, Tarai was made a separate district under a Superintendent. In 1870, Kashipur pargana was restored to the Tarai. On 15th October, 1891, Nainital district came into existence and this District included the Tarai. Regulation IV of 1876 provides that the Tarai district shall not be subjected to :

(a) the jurisdiction of the Courts of Civil judicature constituted by the Regulation of the Bengal Code and by the Acts passed by the Governor General in Council ;

(b) the system of procedure prescribed by the said Regulations and Acts for the said Courts of Civil jurisdiction and Courts of revenue;

(c) the jurisdiction of control of the Courts or Ofice of the revenue constituted by the said regulations and Acts ;

(d) the civil jurisdiction of the High Court of judicature for the north western province.

It further prescribed rules for the trial of Civi suits for the trial of revenue suits, regular and summary, and for the transfer by the local Government of any civil or revenue suits or appeal from any of the local courts to the High Court of judicature for the North-Western provinces or to any other Court in the North-Western Provinces. In civil and revenue cases, an appeal lies to the Commissioner of Kumaon and in criminal cases the courts are under the supervision of the High Court of judicature for the North-Western Provinces.

VIII

The land management can be described as follows :

(a) The Tarai Bhabar was administered as a Government estate by a Superintendent, who enjoyed powers similar to that of a Special Manager, Court of Wards. This post was abolished in 1957 and the Deputy Commissioner Nainital was made responsible for the superintendence and administration of the estate.

(b) The Government estate covering both Tarai and Bhabar areas of Nainital district sprawled over an area of roughly 1,629 square miles with a length of 75 miles and an width ranging between 16 and 25 miles.

The Government estates in Tarai Bhabar comprised the following types of villages :

1. Khan Villages .. 711
2. Buxari villages .. 55
3. Hissedari villages .. 85
4. Thekedari villages .. 35

5. Mustagiri villages .. 53
6. Collonization villages .. 175
7. Mufti villages .. two whole and 19 part villages.

IX

The Tarai-Bhabar area, especially the Tarai, was sparsely populated before independence because of its deadly climate and depredations of wild animals. In the Tarai too, though the land is fertile and rents are small, nothing could overcome the terrible nature of the climate in the east and the Bhoksas, who alone seem to be able to stand its effects, are generally in prosperous circumstances. The immigrants from the plains would no doubt be able to considerable wealth if they only had time to do so, but unfourtunately few of them can live to enjoy the fruits of their labour as their health invariabley fails after a short stayal there and their condition becomes generally most unenviable. Everything possible is done to keep these valuable tenants (Jharus and Buxas) satisfied, for they are the mainstream of cultivation in parts of the Tarai in which no plainsman can live. Government of India Act of 1935 appointed a Committee under the chairmanship of Dr. K. N. Katju, the then Minister for Law and Justice. Another committee was appointed in 1938, chaired by P. W. Marsh, Senior Member, Board of Revenue, to enquire into administration of Government Estates. In 1946, yet another high power committee was constituted under the Chairmanship of Govind Ballabh Pant to report on the development of Tarai-Bhabar.

1. On the recommendations of these committee, the U.P. Government took a number of measures to develop the area and attract outsiders to settle there.

2. In 1948, the Government started their first colonization scheme in the Tarai with the help of World Health Organisation. Effective steps were taken to rid the area of Malaria-the feel disease responsible for taking a heavy toll of human life every year.
3. State and Central Tractor Organization were able to level and bring vast areas, hitherto lying fallow and covered with forest, under the plough.
4. A number of metalled roads were soon built. It goes to the credit of U.P. Government that the area, which was once considered by British as incapable of being developed and habitable by the plainsmen, was colonized and developed into a granery of the State, in less than 15 years after independence.
5. To start with refugees from West Pakistan and erstwhile East Pakistan were settled in the Tarai soon.
6. The Panjabees (including Haryanamen of today) were settled in Tarai.
7. The Government also offered land to freedom fighters, retired army personnel as well as agricultural graduates, who are now counted among the progressive and prosperous farmers of Tarai.
8. Some plainsmen of U.P. have also been settled.
9. Tarai-Bhabar, therefore, has a cosmopolitan population today representing Sikhs, Punjabis, men from U.P., Paharis and plainsmen from several other parts of U.P.

X

The extent of migration in Nainital district can very well be imagined from the following figures of density of population.

Table 4:2

Density of Population

Year	Nainital	U.P.	Percentage in	
			Nainital	U.P.
1921	105	412	—	—
1931	105	439	Nil	6.7
1941	111	498	5.3	13.7
1951	127	557	14.9	11.8
1961	237	648	86.6	16.3

Thus, it is abundantly clear that during 1951-1961, the population of Tarai nearly doubled. The cultivated area in Tarai-Bhabar correspondingly as will be seen from the following figures :

Year	Area under cultivation
1910	624,904
1920	496,592
1958-59	2,174,075
1959-60	2,222,062
1960-61	2,411,687

After independence, the Government Estate of Tarai was arranged in the following order :

1. In Khan villages, the State Government was the proprietor. The U.P. Tenancy Act was in forece. It made rights of the losses inheritable, under rule 4 of the Rules relating to the Management of Government Estates. The Khan tenants had a right to extension-they could bring waste lands adjoining their fields under their plough.
2. The U.P. Tenancy Act did not extend to the Buxari villages. Buxas were allowed shifting cultivation and were recorded in class X(L) of

the Khatauni. As 13 of Buxari villages were acquired for colonization, their number was reduced to 42.

3. As for Hessedari villages, they had intermediaries the Zamindars. U.P. Tenancy Act was not applicable to them.

4. In Thekedari villages, land was leased out to Thekedars for 36 years with right to sublet, but not to transfer the period of lease being renewed for a further term of 30 years.

5. The Mustajirs of Mustajiris, who had the right to let out, mortgage or donate land, had to pay a fixed rent to the Government.

6. In Colonized villages, the State Government exercised property rights. The tenents had hereditary rights and U.P. Tenancy Act was applicable. The lease terms and conditions encouraged cooperative farming.

7. Manfi villages had intermediaries, like the Hissedari village. The U.P. Land Revenue Act was applicable to these villages.

XI

Land management has distinctive categories. They are as follows :

1. In the Khan villages, the State Government was the proprietor under the Government.... Acts. The U.P. Tenancy Act was in force. It made rights of the leases inheritable. Under rule 4 of the Rules relating to the management of Government Estates, the Khan tenants had a right of extension. They could bring waste lands adjoining their fields under their plough.

2. The U.P. Tenancy Act did not extend to the Buxari villages. Buxas were allowed shifting cultivation right and were recorded in class

X(L) of the Khatauni. As 13 of the Buxari villages were acquired for colonization, their number was reduced to 42.

3. With the promulgation of the Zamindari Abolition of Land Reforms Act in 1969, all these categories including distinctive Buxari villages were terminated as follows :

a. Leasees with transferable rights and the land holders have become 'Bhumidars'.

b. Leasees with only heritable right have been classed as 'sirdars'

c. Sub-tenants of disabled persons of retired army-men have been made Asamis.

d. Sub-tenants of able bodied persons have been categoriesed as Adivasis.

Although Bhoksas practiced shifting cultivation in the past, yet their agricultural economy came in force in 1969, i.e., after U.P. Land Reforms Act was promulgated. After 1969, they were forced to settle in a place. Group ownership of land was abolished. They became the owner of lands in the following categories.

(i) Lessees with transferable rights and land holders have become Bhumidars.

(ii) Lessees with only heritable right have seen classed as Sirdars.

(iii) Sub-tenants of disabled persons of retird army-men have been made Asamis.

(iv) Sub-tenants of able bodied persons have been categorised as Adivasis.

Table 4:3 shows the distribution of lands in the village. From the table it is found that the total lands held by theBhoksas of 12 villages in the two districts are 2,481,53 acres of which 2,227,03 acares are irrigated land and 254.5 acres are dry or

Table 4 : 3

Land distribution of the Village in acres

District	Villages	Dry Land	Irrigated Land	Total
Nainital	Beria	—	227.5	227.5
	Birpur	–	56.5	56.5
	Pipal Sanna	104.5	190.00	294.5
	Rajpur	—	198.00	198.00
	Thari	—	226.00	226.00
	Bhuri	—	345.75	345.75
	Khumbadi	—	429.50	429.50
	Sinhali	—	276.00	276.00
	Vikampuri	—	169.00	169.00
Dehra Dun	Tiparpur	131.52	39.96	171.48
	Midnapur & Badripur	—	68.25	68.25
	Mehuwala Khalsa	19.5	—	19.5
	Total :	254.5	2.227.03	2481.53

Table 4 : 4

Generation-wise gradation of land holdings

District	Villages	Members				
		First	Second	Third	Fourth	Total
Nainital	Beria	112	26	—	—	138
	Birpur	6	—	—	—	6
	Pipal Sanna	117	34	3	—	154
	Rajpur	107	35	—	—	142
	Thari	119	33	—	—	152
	Bhuri	218	75	5	—	298
	Khumbadi	199	55	14	2	270
	Sinhali	118	10	—	—	128

District	Villages	Members				
		First	Second	Third	Fourth	Total
Dehra Dun	Vikampuri	62	17	—	—	79
	Tiparpur	560	134	—	—	694
	Midnapur & Badripur	52	18	—	—	70
	Mehuwala Khalsa	137	20	—	—	157
	Total :	1797	457	22	2	2278

unirrigated lands. In general, Nainital Bhoksas have own more lands than that of Dehra Dun Bhoksas. Among the studied villages of Nainital district, Bhoksas of the Khumbari villages held maximum 429.5 acres of land, followed by Bhuri, i.e., 345.7 acres, Pipal Sanna 294.5 acres, Sinhali 276 acres, etc. respectively. Land of Bhoksa inhabited villages of Nainital district are mostly irrigated, with some exceptions, whereas most of the areas in Tiparpur and Mehuwala villages are dry. This agriculture mainly depend on nature, except in some areas on which irrigation is possible, and also in the lands of Medinipur and Badripur.

Table 4:4 shows the generation for which the Bhoksas held land. From the table it is found that out of the 12 studied villages, only two families are holding lands in their name. From the 4th generation some other villages, such as, Pipal Sanna, Bhuri and Khumbari, there are members of families who held land in their names from their 3rd generation, and others are holding lands from very recent times, i.e., either by their father or they themselves acquired and registered the lands in their names from the Land Revenue Office.

From Table 4:5, showing land-holding per family, it is found that families of the area are classified into four categories, i.e., landless, those who have no land in their possession and mostly live as agricultural labour and other kinds of labours. Marginal cultivators, who have very small area of lands in their possession and their liveli-hood dependends on agriculture and agricultural labour. Small land-holding categories, i.e., those who have 2-5 acres of land in their possession, though they depend mainly on land but maintain their families through their hard labour in their fields and survive on the field products. And big farmers, mostly having lands of 6-16 acres. They have to take the help of the community people to cultivate their lands, in preparation of fields and to collect the products of the fields. They mostly depend on labour for their products from the fields.

Table 4:6 shows that Nainital Bhoksa are dependent on only agriculture, but those who are landless or have little land also stick to the traditional occupation of agriculture or agricultural labour. But Bhoksa of Dehradun district are doing a lot of other works to subsist. It is also found that a good number of people adopted sericulture along with their agriculture. Similarly, they are also doing some other works, i.e., collecting materials to prepare soap, selling wood, or selling leaf plate collected from the forest. So, changes in the occupational pattern is found only among the families living in Dehradun district.

XII

a. There are dry lands in the village, but the total area of the village has been encompassed within the facilities of irrigation project.

b. Most of the members of the Bhoksa families are in the habit of borrowing, as so they get themselves indebted either to an institution or to a person. They expose themselves or keep themselves vulnerable to indebtedness for meeting the expenses on various accounts, specially connected with religious and social pursuits and obligations, and, in fact, indebted is due to its origin from demands.

c. Marriage in the society of Bhoksa is an expensive affair and a sense of prestige is attached to it. In order to upkeep the social prestige in solemnising marriages of their wards, they spend beyond their financial limit. Thus, indebtedness became inevitable.

d. Even today, they have to be involve into indebtedness. But the striking feature is that they now approach the SBI and LDB, instead of Benyas, and further we can pinpoint in this regard the purpose of such borrowing as not on marriage and maintenance of social prestige only, but on the purchase of pumping set, bullock, etc., which are too frequent for betterment of their economic status. So, the social status is now grounded on economic upliftment.

e. In the economic field, the setting up of Copperative is a unique attempt and is of utmost importance. It provides short term loan for the purchase of wherewithals and the needs which are specifically required for agricultural activities. Thus, the loan coming from such institutions is contractual and specifically purposive for direct investment.

Chapter - Five

SOCIAL ORGANISATION

I

The Bhoksas are an endogamous group. The existing social organisation among the Bhoksas is of Murdock's Guinea type, which is characterised by exogamous patrilineal kin groups and cousin terminology of Hawaiain types which have evolved patrilineal descent on the basis of patrilocal residence. This society is again segmented into a number of groups. These groups are commonly called as 'gott', or 'gotras' which is equivalent to clan. Names of these 'gotts' are perhaps derived from the names of some renowned personalities of the community, after the name of the original settlement of the past, or after the name of some caste groups. According to Amir Hasan (1971), names of these tribes (gotras) indicate considerable mixture with other classes (Hasan 1971, ibid 56), both Rajput and Brahman (Crook's 56). The 'gott' among them is an expension of the family. The 'gott' members, who are of about the same age, considered each other as brothers (gotti-bhai) and sisters (gotti-bahin). The gott stresses the relationship through one side of the family and claims the superficial blood ties among the gott members which cannot be traced geneologically Elliot (1896. Vol. p. 56) describes them as having fifteen sects (gotras) of which twelve are superior and three are inferior, so far as the rank or hierarchy is concerned. The superiors, according to his list, are Badjugar, Taaleri, Barhanai, Jalwar, Adhoi, Upadhya, Chouhaun, Dauwaria etc. The three inferior clans are Dimar Rather (descended from Teli women), Dhangra (from a hill women) and Goli (from a woman of the barbar caste (Crooks 1989. Vol. II P. 55). And during the Census of 1931, all the clans reported by Elliot, except Dugugiya, Upadhya and Chouhan were found among the Bhoksas of Nainital. (C.I. 1931. Vol. XVIII, Part I, P. 588). But Bhattacharya (1957) reports fourteen gotras, eleven belonging to superior groups and 3 to the inferior groups. But ten superior gotra names given by her differ from those reported by Elliot. Then names of the 10 superior gotras given by Bhattacharya include Panwar and Rajbanshi, which have not been mentioned by Elliot. On the other hand, Badjugar, Taaleri, Barhanai, Nagauria and Jalal gotras mentioned by Elliot do not find place in the list of gotras furnished by Bhattacharya. (Bhattacharya 1957, Vanyajati Vol. V, No. 4 P.P. 184, 185 :) According to 1961 Census, Vol. I, Part V.B (IV), field work conducted among the Bhoksa of Nainital district it was found that the distinction between superior gotras has no practical implications in social relations among the members of the community in the matter of regulating marital relations. In the two villages, where the field investigatnion was carried out, the following names of gotras were reported : Agarwal (Mehtar-Bania), Gaindola, Chimmal, Gulzarpuria, Jogipuria, Rajauria, Dalwariya, Bhikampuria and Baruwere. It is seen that the names of gotras recorded during the present survey are in many cases different from those reported by earlier scholars. "From the examination of the names of these gotras, it is found that except Agarwal, Chimmal and Bargupar, others derive their names from the various villages in the three Tahsils of Nainital" (Census 1961).

Here, it requires mentioning that Bhoksas of Nainital district put more emphasis on Khera, the place of their original habitat, than that of gotras. This Khera is exogamous in marriage alliances. It is believed that member of the same Khera is the descendant of the same family. According to Hasan Amir (1979) : it is found :

> ... that many Bhoksas do not remember their gotras and quote their Khera as their gotra. There are yet others who confuse the two and quote gotras in place of Khera and vice versa. It appears that the concept of Khera is pronounced only in district Nainital. The Bhoksas of Dehra Dun does not appear to have clear concept of Khera. Even in many villages of Nainital district, people do not differentiated between Kheras and gotras.

He refers to the following gotras in Dehradun and Bijor districts, Viz., Hardia, Bhatta Pawar, Badgujar, Doi, Rai, Jagatdeopawar, Muswani, Chouhan, Vaishya, Mundia Bhaur Bhatti, Betwal, Gaur, Katwal, Dandwal. But he refered both gotras and Khera of Nainital Bhoksas to provide a clear picture of the concept of Khera or gotras.

Table 5 : 1

Gotra-Khera Particular

Gotras	Kheras
Dandbaria/Dahdavaria	Dhakiyua
Kanjoia	Dharavala
Joga	Kanetawala
Khurfria	Siariawala/Siariware

Gotras	Kheras
Chamar	Urwaria
Nahi	—
Nigoria	—
Nigodia/Negauria	Chankairai
Teli	Hastan
Nai	Khawariawnla
Jalal	Ghuriwala
Rathanr	Kopawala
Jalahe	Jurka
Dhangaria	Katra Kutra Powalgwalia
	Tara Khera Partapuria
	Singh Garha Suhaliwalc
	Sisawala Itwayya
	Noholiwala Gulyarpuia
	Nandpuia Gulzarpuia

Table 5 : 2

In the present study, the following Kheras are reported from a villages of Nainital district.

Gotras	Khera
1. Gujar	Motkotia
	Biopuria
Semial	Kopawala
2. Bar Gujar Jamal	Kopa
	Shisona
	Sikarpuria
	Vikampuria
	Moliwalay
	Dehradun

	Chapka
	Kultri Kurta
3. Ahir	Khempuria
4. Zalal	Barnawala
5. Chouhan	Melpuria
6.	Gogipuria
	Ambaria
	Gogiwala
7. Kashayap	Vikaupuria
	Gogiwara
	Dangulia
	Sakatpuria
	Mitibare
	Darbaria Vhoselpuria
8. Thawal	Banoa Khera
9. Paidar	Naiwalaya
	(Khotaua)
10. Dogra	
11. Mahato Bania	
12. Kamra	
13. Domra	
14. Nagaria	
15. Dhangria	

The sub-group names mentioned in Table 5 : 2 are considered as Gott by the Bhoksas of Nainital district. Among these sub-groups, the Darbaria and Bargujar have two Khera.

The sub-group or gott Darabaria has two Kheras, viz. Mitibari and Khosalpuria. It is said by the members of Darbaria sub-group that founder of two villages, i.e., Khosalpuria and Mitibari were two

	Bar-Gujar Dehradun	Ahir	Darbaria	Kamdevpuria	Sakatpuria	Vikampuria	Daunguria	Beruawala
Birpur	1	—	—	—	1	—	—	—
Pipal Sanna	7	4	7	1	—	1	1	1
Rajpur	12	4		—	2	1	—	1
Thari	—		6	—	—	14	—	1
Bhuri	6	1	23	3	5	—	—	2
Khumbari	11	—	8	—	—	2	2	2
Sinhali	2	—	2	—	—	—	—	—
Vikampuri	5	—		—	5	9	—	4
Tiparpur	—	—	—	—	—	—	—	—
Medinipur & Badripur	—	—	—	—	—	—	—	—
Mehuwala Khalsa	—	—	—	—	—	—	—	—

	Pipal Sanna	Madan puria	Kamara	Chininwala	Singiwala	Thawala	Simal	Motkotia	Pawal garia
Birpur	—	—	—	—		—	—	—	—
Pipal Sanna	2	2	4	—					
Rajpur						3			
Thari	1					1	1	3	
Bhuri	—	6					2	—	1
Khumbari	—	—	3	5	1	1	12	—	—
Sinhali									
Vikampuri									
Tiparpur									
Medinipur & Badripur									
Mehuwala Khalsa									

	Boniare	Chou rasia	Mahato Bania	Gujar	Gadaria	Guljar-puria	Cham-bawal	Chouhan	Toumur
Birpur		3							
Pipal Sanna						5			
Rajpur						5			
Thari									
Bhuri			2						
Khumbari			2			1			
Sinhali				22	2				
Vikampuri									
Tiparpur							33	31	26
Medinipur & Badripur							5	2	—
Mehuwala Khalsa							5	5	3

	Malan has	Pundir	Kakar	Falsana	Baufan	Chad	Tejwar	Laxiwala	Nagina	Pundir (Nai)
Birpur										
Pipal Sanna										
Rajpur										
Thari										
Bhuri										
Khumbari										
Sinhali										
Vikampuri										
Tiparpur	23	22	17						4	2
Medinipur & Badripur	3	4	7	16	3					
Mehuwala Khalsa		3	—	14	—	2	10	1	—	—

6

brothers. They settled in different villages with their relatives. Although they are recognized as a Khosalpuria and Mitibare, giving much stress on their present settlement, yet they were actually the members of the same gott, i.e., Darbaria. These two groups are exogamous in marriage selection. Similarly, in the case of Bargujar there are two sections-Semial and Jamal, with reference to their past settlement of Motkotia.

From the present work, 12 villages of two districts have been studied. Thus, there are altogether 36 clans. Out of these 36 clans or gotras of Kheras, 24 clans or Kheras are available in 9 villages of Nainital district and the rest 12 gotras are found in the villages of Dehradun district. In Nainital district, the clan groups of Darbaria is forming the major groups of the studied villages. It is seconded by the Bargujar clan. And groups like Thawal is having the minimum population in these villages. The other groups have a considerable number in those villages. Similarly, in the district of Dehradun, Chambal groups is forming the major clan group of the area, wheras the Laxmiwal group is having the minimum population in the village. The rest of the other groups have a considerable number in the studied villages.

II

In the Bhoksa society, lineage is found. It is a part of social structure, though the lineage groups include the married sisters and daughters and exclude wives of male lineage members. Members of a lineage group may be recognized through their action. It is customary that the members of a lineage must mourn in thecase of death of any lineage member and in the case of others of the lineage he

Table 5:3 Distribution of Gotras in the studied villages.

	Beria	Birpur	Pipal Sanna	Rajpur	Thari	Bhuri	Kham-Badi	Sinhali	Vikam-Puri	Tipar-Pur	Medini Pur & Badri-pur	Mehuw-ala Khalsa
Bargujar	F	F	F	F	—	F	F	F	F	—	—	—
Ahir	—	—	F	—	F	—	—	—	—	—	—	—
Darbaria	F	—	F	—	F	F	F	F	—	—	—	—
Kamdevpuria	F	—	F	F	—	F	—	—	—	—	—	—
Sakatpuria	—	—	F	F	—	F	—	—	F	—	—	—
Daunguria	F	—	F	—	—	—	F	—	—	—	—	—
Beruwawala	F	—	F	F	F	F	F	—	—	—	—	—
Pachula	—	—	F		F							
Madanpuria	F	—	F			F						
Kamora							F					
Chininwala							F					
Simiriwala	F			F	F	—	F					
Thawal							F					
Simal		F				F	F					
Motkotia					F							
Pawalguria	F					F						

	Beria	Birpur	Pipal Sanna	Rajpur	Thari	Bhuri	Kham-Badi	Sinhali	Vikam-Puri	Tipar-Pur	Medini Pur & Badri-pur	Mehuw-ala Khalsa
Bouara	F											
Chourasia		F										
Mahato-Bania						F	F					
Gujar								F				
Gudaria								F				
Guljarpuria	F	F	—	F	F	—	F	—				
Chambawal										F	F	F
Chouhan										F	F	F
Toumour										F	—	F
Malanhas										F	F	—
Pundir										F	F	F
Kakar										—	F	F
Falsana												F
Banfan												F
Chad												F
Tejwar												F
Laximiwal												F
Nagina												F
Pundir (nai)										F	—	—

becomes ritually polluted, generally for 13 days. On the 13th day, after death of the member, the lineage member assemble for purificatory function. They bathe and wash their clothes. The preist is called to perform purificatory rites. Sometimes a close lineage relative is permitted to observe the rites for a son, if the deceased person has no son; secondly, the lineage group as a segment of sib or clan is strictly exogamous. A woman can have sex relations with her husband's brothers, real and classificatory, but never with the people of her own lineage. When a woman is widowed or divorced, she either can marry her husband's brother-a subsequent marriage can be arranged with reference to her parents-in-laws lineage, because her sib or clan is considered as exogamous. Thirdly, the lineage group plays also a major role in the affairs of property. As the Bhoksa woman has no right to the lands, so, in case the family has no male child, the property will be held by the lineage group collectively. The lineage member who performs all the death rites of the deceased person may get the property of the dead person, or sometimes this property is held as lineage or clan members' property by the chief of the clan. A gott-head becomes the traditional leader and his Khandan or lineage groups are his allies. The relatives, consangunial as well as affinal, support him at any time when they are in need of such support. When the support of them is needed by him, he gets it. These groups have also played an important role in marriage alliances also. Generally, the Khandan members or relatives of Khandan do the match-making. They extend their support to their lineage or clan members on different occasions, such as, marriage, birth, death, etc.

III

Marriage within the gott is forbidden by the Bhoksas. As they consider *gotti* or clan members as brothers / sisters claiming their origin from the same ancestor. They consider *gotts* as close kins and prohibition of marriage within these groups which is also imposed by them. These groups are ;

(1) *Dada Raya* - Lineage of grand-father.

(2) *Nana Raya* - Lineage of meternal grandfather.

(3) *Damad Raya* - Lineage of in-laws and

(4) *Devti Raya* - Lineage of grand children.

The prohibition is also imposed in the step-father's or step-mother's lineage. All these relative are considered prohibitory to them. The prohibition is also imposed in the step-fatehr's or step-mother's lineage. All these relatives are within the frame-work or prohibition, incest as they are considered as *Bhatti* (Rice giver or taker groups). On every occasion, such as death, birth and especially at the time of marriage, they have to be called in. They will provide their support according to their capacity. But it is the convention that, if any group after receiving information, will not be present or give their gifts on such an occasion, they do not get a meal from those houses.

Table : 5:4 shows the Preference of alliances among clans or gotras of the studied villages.

If we consider that exogamy and incest have a permanent functional value, then it may be said that exogamy, on the other hand, assists the social existence of other people, which ensures the integration of partial units within, to total group and demands of the collaboration of outside groups. Thus, it forms a permanent and continual excellence of

Table : 5:4

Nainital	Clan and Marriage Alliances
Bar-Gujar	Baruawala, Kamdevpuria, Sakatpuria.
Ahir	Simiriwala, Pachula, Bar-Gujar, Gujar.
Darbaria	Vikampuria, Guljarpuria, Kamora.
Kamdevpuria	Vikampuria, Pawalgaria.
Vikampuria	Naiwaray, Baruawala, Simiriwala, Guljarpuria, Jogipuria, Darbaria, Khosalpuria.
Daungarwala	Darbaria, Mahato-bania.
Baruwawalay	Gujar, Sakatpuria, Singniwala.
Pachula	Singniwala, Baruawala.
Madanpuria	Kamdevpuria, Guljarpuria, Boniware.
Kamora	Sakatpuria.
Chinchinwala	Gujar, Ahir.
Singniwala	Guljarpuria, Darbaria, Mahato-Bania.
Thawal	Chad
Simal	Baruwala, Kamdevpuria, Singniwala.
Matkotia	Ahir, Pachula.
Pawalgaria	Darbaria.
Boniware	Baruawala, Mitibare.
Chourasia	Vikampuria.
Mahato-Bania	Ahir, Gujar.
Gujar	Ahir, Vikampuria, Pachula.
Gadaria	Gujar, Simal.
Guljarpuria	Pawalgaria, Simal.

Dehradun District	**Clan and Marriage Alliances**
Tomour	Falsana, Laxmiwal, Pundir, Chambawal, Malanhas, Chouhan, Kakar.
Pundir	Chambawal, Chouhan, Falsana, Tomour, Laxmiwal, Malanhas, Tejwar.

Falsana	Laximwal, Chambawal, Chouhan, Pundir, Chad, Kakar, Malanhas.
Chad	Chambawal, Chouhan.
Chouhan	Tejawan, Tomour, Chambawal, Pundir. Falsana, Kakar Poum.
Tejawan	Chouhan, Tomour.
Chouhan(Nai)	Tejwan.
Chambawal	Falsana, Chouhan, Pundir, Tomour, Malanhas.
Laxmiwal	Chouhan
Kakar	Tomour
Bafan	Chouhan
Ningana	Pundir

adjustment from both biological and social points of view, without which life is impossible. And on the other hand, incest prohibition provides two types of bond :

> That one of them impresses a mechanical solidarity (brother), while other involves an organic solidarity (brother-in-law or godfather). Brothers are closely related to one another.... By contrast, brothers-in-law are solidarity, because they complement each other and have a functional efficacy for one another.... a wife through their simultaneous renunciation of what they both do have a sister. The first form of solidarity add nothing and unites nothing; it is based upon a cultural limit, satisfied by the production of a type of connection, the model for which is provided by nature. The other brings about an integration of the group on a new plan (Levi Stranss : 1949; p. 489).

Some Bhoksas offer their girls to other community, though the number of offeering girls to other community is very insignificant in comparison to the total number of marriage. There are 8 men who offered their daughters to other community. The Bhoksa society does not take this easily. They try to deal with the case in their Panchayat and also try to settle the case amicably, imposing some fine by the father of those girls. Mehra society considered that mere fine of Rs. 25/- or Rs. 100/- is not the only remedy to protect their community from the expected danger, which they are facing due to the deeds by some of their community members, who are otherwise economically sound and also have a good reputation among the outside communities. They withdraw their support from those particular family. The process of withdrawal of their support from those particular family gradually gathers its momentum since they attach more importance on the incident than those clans; families and of personalities of the said community, so they face a social boycott. Those men who offer their girls to other communities as wives face two kinds of problems. Firstly, they give their girls to other community, but this particular community who receive the girl as wives from the Mehra Bhoksa refuses to offer any girl to the Mehras Bhoksas. Similarly, as they are considered guilty of the customs of their community for offering their girls to other community, their community members are reluctant ot offer their girls to those families or to receive in return. Thus, these categories of people found themselves in dilemma. Since they confess their mistake to the clan-heads and register their request to set the problem right, even on payment by way of compensation, because of recognition of their original status is essential for their existence.

IV

Marriage by negotiation is Prevalent among the Bhoksa. The local term of negotiated marriage is *biya* or *sadhi.* Other types of marriage, such as, marriage by exchange, elopement and *gharjamai* marriage are also found among them. But these types are permitted by the society only depending on the special situation. In the case of love affairs, parents of the respective boy and girl take initiative to materialize the marriage through negotiation. Other types of marriage, i.e., marriage by elopment and *gharjamai* marriage are also found in the Bhoksa community. The Bhoksa society also permits pre-puberty marriage as it prevalent among them. In pre-puberty marriage, the age of marriage for a girl is 6 years or more, and that for a boy is 8 to 10 years. It is said that sometimes a marriage is contracted between the prospective in-laws before the birth of their children. At present, generally the marriageable age for the boys varies from 17 to 19 years and for the girls, it is 14 to 18 years. But sometimes this age may be extended on some economic as well as other grounds or on the ground of sudden death of any family members if the *sagai* (betrothal) or *Magni* is completed. Generally, a Brahmin sends the letter to the bride's party mentioning Rashi, Nakshatra of the bride and/or bridegroom. In this letter remedies, if there be any fault, are also suggested to save the expected couple from hazards, which may come in the life of the perspective couple. According to Bhoksas pandit mentions *Ban,* which actually is the bad conjuntion of some stars, as it is revealed in the calculation of the pandit astrologically.

V

Other types of Marriages :

When a boy and a girl fall in love with each other and decide to marry, then the boy conveys his decision to his father through some relatives. Among the Bhoksa, the father generally accepts the proposal of his son and tries to arrange the marriage through negotiation. In the love-cum-social marriage, boy's father generally sends some person to the girl's father with the request for the acceptance of the proposal of marriage. If both the parties are satisfied, then only this marriage is accepted. If both the boy and the girl do not belong to the same gotra or *Khera,* then only this sort of marriage is conducted socially.

The *Gharjamai*-marriage generally takes place when a well-to-do Bhoksa has no son, but has a daughter or daughters. Bhoksa boys do not like to accept the gharjamai marriage, because in gharjamai marriage, a Bhoksa man looses his liberty. So, gharjamai marriage is rare among them. Only in some special cases, when a well-to-do Bhoksa men has only one daughter, and he is a good friend of the father or the boy and he has no one to look after him in his old days, then generally the 'gharjamai' marriage is agreed upon.

Polygny is practised by the Bhoksa, but on very rare occasions. The general tendency among them is to go in for monogamous type of marriage. Generally, if the first wife is barren, then only a man can socially be allowed to marry again and that also with the consent of his first wife. Divorce is permissible in the Bhoksa society. But, generally, a man divorces his wife when she is proved to be of loose character or have a quarrel-some habit. Sterility is not a suitable ground for divorce.

Table 5:6

Types of Marriage

Villages	Negotiation	Elopment	Others	Total
Beria	46	—	—	46
Birpur	13	—	—	13
Pipal Sanna	48	—	—	48
Rajpur	44	—	—	44
Thari	42	—	—	42
Bhuri	73	—	—	73
Khumbari	75	—	—	75
Sinhali	30	—	—	30
Vikampuri	24	—	—	24
Tiparpur	180	11	—	191
Midnapur & Badripur	48	—	—	48
Mehuwala Khalsa	53	—	—	53
Total :	676	11		687
	98.39	(1.61)		100%

Table : 5:6 shows that out of total 687 marriage 98.39 are solomonised through negotiation and the rest 1.6 is of Elopment in nature.

Table 5:7

Forms of Marriage

Villages	Monogamy	Polygamy	Total Marriage
Beria	46	—	46
Birpur	13	—	13
Pipal Sanna	48	—	48
Rajpur	44	—	44
Thari	39	3	42
Bhuri	73	—	73
Khumbari	75	—	75
Sinhali	30	—	30 (in 2 remarriage)
Vikampuri	21	3	24
Tiparpur	187	4	191
Midnapur & Badripur	52	1	53
Mehuwala Khalsa	47	1	48
Total :	675	12	687
	98.23%	1.77%	100%

Table : 5:7 shows that out of total 687 marriage 98.23% marriage are of monogamous in nature and rest 1.77% are polygamous.

Generally, divorce is taken by women. When a women is incapable of adjusting with her husband's family members or she has pre-marital relationship with any other persons, then the girl after marriage, when comes to visit her father's house she won't want to return and the father of the girl also supports her and refuses to send her daughter back to the bridegroom's house and seeks for a divorce. Remarriage of a widow or a divorcee person is permitted by the society. Normally, a young widow or a divorcee always wants a good partner for her or him. Generally among the Bhoksa, parents take initiative for the settlement. If they get a suitable match for their girl or boy, then with the approval of the senior members of the society, even if he or she has children by the previous wife or husband, they arrange for a remarriage.

VI

The Bhoksa society is patriarchal and patrilineal. After marriage, the wife lives in her husband's place. In some exceptional cases, a son-in-law goes to his wife's native place and establishes a separate family there. Table 5:8 gives some examples of change of residence of a groom after marriage. Between the newly married wife and mother or sister the situation compels the groom to go an to settle in the village of his in-laws. And they prefer to go to their wife's village or to father-in-law's residence.

The reasons to shift to in-law's settlement were variously explained by the informant. According to some, the newly married girls generally do not like to go to their husband's residence, if it is located at a distant place. Besides this, there are system of *Gharjamai* , i.e., persons who has the only daughter, would make a contract with the parents of the

Table : 5:8

List of Change of Residences

Name	Birth Place	Present Matri-village Residence
1. Laxman Sing	Madanpuria	Khumbari
2. Shayam Sing	Bhat-Bhog	Khumbari
3. Share Sing	Bhoksa Village (Dineshpur)	Khumbari
4. Mohan Sing	PIpal Sanna	Khumbari
5. Man Sing	Birputra	Khumbari
6. Silla Sing	Baria	Khumbari
7. Bhagh Sing	Banna-Khera	Khumbari
8. Prem Sing	Bajpur	Pipal Sanna
9. Kishan Sing	Gulbar bhose	Pipal Sanna
10. Karma Sing	Birpur Lachi	Pipal Sanna
11. Sobbi Sing	Birpurtara	Pipal Sanna
12. Lachu Sing	Simiriwala	Thari
13. Hari Sing	Banna-Khera	Thari
14. Kishan Sing	Khempuri	Thari
15. Sarup Sing	Bajabala	Thari
16. Dhobi Sing	Bajabala	Thari
17. Tika Sing	Birpurtara	Thari
18. Hero Deri	Khumbari	Sinhali
19. Lasker Sing	Khumbari	badripur (Dehradun)
20. Babu Ram Sing	Signiwala	Tiparpur
21. Ram Sing	Singniwala	Tiparpur
22. Dharm Sing	Singniwala	Tiparpur

Name	Birth Place	Present Matri-village Residence
23. Mukram Sing	Kunja	Tiparpur
24. Dat Ram	Madipura	Tiparpur
25. Ram Dayal	Garitil 1	Tiparpur
26. Pram Sing	—	Tiparpur
27. Man Sing	Barbala	Mehuwala Khalsa
28. Jita Ram	Dhorpur	Mehuwala Khalsa
29. Dobi Ram	Bhurpur	Mehuwala Khalsa
30. Debi Sing	Bambala	Mehuwala Khalsa

bridegroom has to stay with his after marriage. In some cases, it is due to conflict.

VII

The family is a domestic as well as a residential unit of the Bhoksas which consists of a man, his wife or wives, sons and their wifes with unmarried sons and daughters. But every family belongs to one clan or Khera, which is exogamous. Among the Bhoksa, monogamous families are prevalent-one man with one wife, albit some Polygamous types of families are also found, i.e., one man has more than one wives, but their family would never be a polyandrous. Four types of families are found among the Bhoksa, viz., nuclear families, extended families broken families and other families.

Type 1 : A nuclear family consists of a married couple with their children or a married couple without any child. A man with a second wife and children of the first marriage has also been included in the first category of nuclear family.

Type II : The extended type of family is composed of more than one married couple with their unmarried children or parents of the married males.

Type III : A broken family consists of a married couple and their unmarried children together with a widow mother or widower father.

Type IV : The fourth category of family, i.e., the Other type may include members like unmarried and orphaned brothers and sisters living together. Sometimes widowed daughter or divorced daughter

Table : 5 : 9

Types of Family

District	Villages	Nuclear	Extended	Broken	Other	Total
Nainital	Beria	18	11	2	1	32
	Birpur	6	3	—	—	9
	Pipal Sanna	6	10	13	1	30
	Rajpur	9	12	2	1	24
	Thari	11	9	12	4	36
	Bhuri	21	18	4	1	44
	Khumbadi	31	17	7	2	57
	Sinhali	23	3	1	1	28
	Vikampuri	9	6	4	—	19
Dehra Dun	Tiparpur	97	30	30	1	158
	Medinipur & Badripur	26	11	2	1	40
	Mehuwala Khalsa	33	6	3	1	43
Total :		290 (55.8%)	136 (25.8%)	80 (15.1%)	14 (2.3%)	520

Table : 5:9, depicts that nuclear types of families are predomination over the other types of families. They are forming 55.8% and the rest extended families are 25.8% broken families are 15.1% and other types of families are only 2.3%.

along with children may put up with her parents. Sometimes a widower or a divorcee son along with children may live with parents.

Table 5:9 depcits the different types of family.

VIII

Bhoksa kinship system refers to the aggregate of relatives who are closely associated with the families. So, this relationship may be classified according to Murdock, (primary relatives' or those who belong to the same nuclear family of a particular person), namely, his father, mother, sister and brother in his family of orientation and his wife, his sons and his daughters in his family of procreation. Although each of these relatives will have his own primary relatives, most of whom are not included among the primary relatives of the family but may be treated as secondary or tertiary relatives. Most of them are detected or traced at the time of marriage settlement when some of these relations come under incest. Actually, primary 'Kin group which comprises both consanguineal and affinal have their regular interaction in social and economic matters of life. This is codified in the system of terms used by the people in addressing and referring to one another. The Bhoksa kinship terms may be classified as classificatory system, especially the Hawaian type where all the cross and parallel cousins are called by the same terms as those used for sisters and brothers. Although there are denotative and descriptive types of kinship, a list of kinship terms and terms of address are given below. Two separate columns are also given in interpreting the kinship terms of two districts to show the kind of difference that may take place in the kinship terms of the Bhoksas living in the two districts.

Table : 5:10

Kinship terminology of the Bhoksas of Nainital and Dehra dun district.

Sl. no.	English term	Term used by the Nainital Bhoksa	Term of address by the Nainital Bhoksa	Term used by the Dehra Dun Bhoksa	Term of address by the Dehra Dun Bhoksa
1	2	3	4	5	6
1.	Father's father	Dadda	Dadara	Dadda	Dadaji
2.	Mother's father	Nanna	Nannara	Nanna	Nannaji
3.	Father's mother	Daddi	Dadira	Dadi	Dadie
4.	Mother's mother	Nanni	Nannira	Nanni	Nannie
5.	Father	Abba	Abbara	Pita	Pitaji
6.	Mother	lea	leari	Meta	Ma
7.	Father's elder brother	Toue	Tauery	Toue	Touji
8.	Father's younger brother	Chacha	Chachara	Chacho	Chachoji
9.	Father's elder brother's wife	Taie	Taieari	Tai	Tai
10.	Father's younger brother's wife	Kaki	Kakira	Chachi	Chachiji
11.	Father's elder sister	Phuphu	Phuphuri	Phuphi	Phuphiji
12.	Father's younger sister	Phuphu	Phuphuri	Phuphi	Phuphiji
13.	Father's elder sister's husband	Phupha	Phuphaji	Phupha	Phuphaji
14.	Mother's brother	Mammu	Mammuji	Mamma	Mammaji

1	2	3	4	5	6
15.	Mother's brother's wife	Mai	Mairay	Mammi	Mammaji
16.	Mother's elder sister	Barie	Bariarie	Moushi	Moushie
17.	Mother's younger sister	Moushi	Moushiary	Moushi	Moushie
18.	Mother's elder sister's husband	Borha	Borhaji	Mousha	Moushaji
19.	Mother's younger sister' husband	Mousha	Moushariy	Mousha	Moushaji
20.	Wife's father	Shashar	Podhan	Sashar	
21.	Wife's mother	Shash	Buria	Shash	
22.	Elder brother (m s)	Adda	Addari	Bhaia	Bhaia
23.	Younger brother (m s)	Bhaia	Bhaiara	Choto Bhai	Bhaia
24.	Elder brother (w s)	Jhet		Jhet	
25.	Younger brother (w b)	Debar	By name	Debar	By name
26.	Younger sister (m s)	Bahen	By name	Nanadh	By name
27.	Younger sister (w s)	Nanadh	"	Nanadh	"
28.	Father's elder brother' son	Bhaia	"	Bhaia	"
29.	Father's younger brother's son	Bhaia	"	Bhaia	"
30.	Father's elder brother's daughter	Bahin	"	Bahin	"
31.	Father's younger brother' daughter	Bahin	"	Bahin	"
32.	Father's sister's son	Bhanja	"	Bhanja	"

1	2	3	4	5	6
33.	Father's sister's daughter	Bhanji	"	Bhanji	"
34.	Husband (w. s)	Log (Khasam)	—	Pati	—
35.	Wife (m.s)	Gharawali	—	Garawali	—
36.	Wife's younger sister	Sali	By name	Sali	By name
37.	Wife's elder sister	Baralia	—	Sali	—
38.	Wife's elder sister's husband	Sarhu	By name	Sarhu	By name
39.	Wife's younger sister's husband	Sarhu	By name	Sarhu	By name
40.	Husband's younger brother's wife	Jathani	—	Jathani	—
41.	Elder sister's husband	Bhonhai	By name	Bhonhai	By name
42.	Elder sister' husband (w s)	Nandhai	—	Nandhi	—
43.	Son's wife's father	Samandhi	—	Samandhi	—
44.	Son's wife's mother	Samandhan	—	Samandhan	—
45.	Younger brother's son	Bhatija	By name	Bhatija	By name
46.	Elder brother's son	Bhatija	"	Bhatija	—
47.	Elder brother's daughter	Bhatiji	"	Bhatiji	"
48.	Younger brother's daugher	Bhatiji	"	Bhatiji	"
49.	Daughter's husband	Damad	Jamai	Damad	Jamai
50.	Son's wife	Bahu	Bahurai	Bahu	Bahu

1	2	3	4	5	6
51.	Son' son	Pota	By name	Potta	By name
52.	son's daughter	Potti	"	Potti	"
53.	Son's son's son	Potta Debata	"	Debta	"
54.	Daughter's son	Debta	By name	Debta	By name
55.	Daughter's daughter	Debti	"	Debti	"
56.	Daughter's daughter's daughter	Poti Devti	"	Pota Debti	"
57.	Father's fatehr's father	Par Dada	—	Par Dada	—
58.	Father's fathers' mother	Par Daddi	—	Par Daddi	—
59.	Step mother	Mousi	—	Mousi	—
60.	Step father	Chacha	—	Chacha	—

From table 4:6 kinship terms and addresses, it is found that all the primary relatives, i.e., father, mother, sister and brother in a Bhoksa family of orientation and an individual's wife or her husband, his son and his daughter in his family of procreation is used as a single kinship category and identified only as one person, i.e., ego in denotative term. This denotative term is also extended to secondary kinship categories, like Fa FA, FaMo, MoFa, MoMo, FaSi, MoSi, FaBr, etc. And in the case of some secondary kinship categories, like FaSo, FaDa, MoSo, BrWi, BrSo, BrDa, etc. are extended forms of the terms originally denoting some primary relatives to one or more categories of secondary orremoteer kinsmen categories by applying a distinctive term to several categories of secondary term. But some of the secondary kinships are also classed under the classificatory kinship groups. And tertiary categories, including eight great grand parents, eight first cousin, the spouses of all uncles and aunts, nephews and nieces and many other distant relatives are classified as classificatory groups. It requires mentioning here that teknonymy is found prevalent in the case of husband and wife as in general females or males do not call their wives/males in any kinship term. They call the respective wife or husband mentioning the father or son or daughter.

IX

Pattern of inter-personal relationship between different relatives can better be judged through the study of inter-personal relations that knits the relatives into a pattern/design.

Table 5:11

Categories of Behavioural patern

Respect	...	Fa, Mo, ElBr, Si, FaEib Br, FaYeBr, MoSi.
Reserved	...	ElBr, Yo Br, Hu, Mo, HuFa, WiFa, WiMo, HuEiSi, WiElSi, WiElSi, HuElBr, MoBr, ElDa, FaelSi, Da, DaHu, FaBr So.
Informal	...	FaFa, MoFa.
Intimate	...	ElSiHu, FaSiSo, MoBrSo, WiBr, SiHu, MoSiSo, FaBrDa, MoSiDa, HuBrWi, SoWiMo, DaHuMo, DaHuMo, Da.
Avoidance	...	HuFa, YoBrWi, HuElBr, DaHu, SoWi, WiMo, WiFa, FaElSi.
Jocking	...	SonSo, DaSo, SiDa, SoDa MrBrYoDa, FaYo, SiDa, ElBrWi, WiSi, Hu Yo Si, Wi, Hu Yo Br.

Husband and wife

Marriage is a social bondage that inspires them to commence their conjugal life. Conjugal life is nothing but the adjustment of husband and wife. Generally the husband earns and the wife manages the household duties. In all the socio-religious activities, husband's opinion as well as wife's opinion are accepted in the social life. The husband discusses with his wife matters concerning their family. In the economic life, husband and wife are co-partners. Besides this, wife prepares food, does nourishing of children, household works and also helps her husband in the field in carrying out agricultural operations, such as, weeding, transplanting, harvesting, etc. In Dehradun district, Bhoksa women also help her husband in the work of making rope as well as in sericultural work. The wife always looks after the welfare of her husband and the family members. The husband also takes care about wife's health, if she falls ill. Sometimes if any conflict arises, due to some disagreement between them, it leads to divorce. Main cause of divorce is the pre and post marital sex-links with other women or men respectively in the case of husband and wife. Sometimes barrenness, sexual offence, disease and other reasons contribute to the cause towards the formation of main conflicts between husband and wife. But generally, husband does not nurse the idea of divorcing a woman because she is one of the active working members of the family. When barrenness of women is the main cause of conflict, then women generally permit the husband to marry again. Hence, we find how economic force covers the moral lapses, but the departure of the rule is that, when the conflict crops up resting on the point of barrenness of the women, permission is accorded to husband to project himself for a second marriage. But such cases are very rare among the Bhoksa.

Father and son

Father and son are good friends to each other. They work together in the field and also participate in other works that are within the ambit of the family. The father acts as a friend, philosopher, guide and trainer to his son. In social activities, however, when father recedes at the dictation of age, the son gets into his shoes as a representative of the family. Generally, the son obeys his father's authority. The father cuts jokes with his grown up sons as friends, addressing the son as 'yaar'. They smoke sitting together and gossip. They also discuss about the family problems as well as other socio-economic factors. In their custom, the son inherits the property. So, generally sons obey the orders of the father. The married sons sometimes start a new household. But they extend their assistance to parents in every possible affairs. At the same time, the father helps them considerably in getting them settled. Power of authority still clings to the person of the father, but the son discharges the function in obedience to the advice of his father. Their relationship is so close and friendly that it may be stretched to that point of freedom and easiness to address each other as 'yaar'.

Father and daughter

Relationship between father and daughter is saturated with the feeling of affection. She takes care of the father at the time of illness and also in every details of his day-to-day life. Father feels the responsibility of putting her into marriage. Even after marriage he always keeps contact with her. He is always sympathetic about his daughter and her family. He makes necessary arrangement for the welfare of her daughter's family. In case of any sort of conflict between the daughter and son-in-law, the girl's father always takes the side of his daughter. In case of divorce or widowhood of daughter, father brings her back to his place and either keeps her within his family or arranges for her re-marriages.

Mother and son

Mother and son relation is marked with the feelings of affection. As the son is the future head as well as future guide of the family, mother always takes care of her male child. A grown up child is the nucleus of the family. The son wide opens his wings to give shelter to his mother and shields the family which his father did previously. She can even do worst things for the welfare of her son. At the same time, the son respects her and stands by her in all contingencies of life, specially in old age. The wife of the son acts resembling her husband towards the mother-in-law. She obeys her directives even in socio-religious pursuits. After the son's birth, mother looks over the child. She is always alert about his sons health. She won't tolerate anybody to touch it who hurts her child. She rears up her son by her own breast milk, and carries him about to pull him to sleep. The son looks after his mother and takes care at the time of her illness. If he is married, his wife is also expected to respect and obey her in the matter of family and in other socio-religious aspects.

Mother and daughter

Mother and daughter relation is very affectionate. The feeling of the mother towards her daughter is quite similar to that of her son. A young daughter is co-worker to her mother. She looks after the household with her mother and takes part in the agricultural operations, such as, weeding, transplantation, threshing with her mother. At the same time, she helps her mother in preparing food, fetching drinking water from the tubewell, etc. She looks after her young brothers and sisters and also feeds them. For a young girl, her mother is her guide. Mother trains her daughter about household work, so that she may not face any difficulty in her husband's house. The mother plays most significant role in the training of her daughter as in the case of the father for the son.

Brother and Brother

Brothers are co-workers and have an affectionate feeling for each other, but the elder one usually dominates over younger ones. Brothers play together, rejoice together and also quarrel among themselves. In the family, they work together under the instruction of their father. They go to the field for cultivation and help their father in maintaining the family. whenever the younger brother is asked about any socio-economic aspect of the family, he generally refers it to his elder brother. The brothers have economic cooperation among them. At the same time, they are the main conflicting parties. The brothers quarrel and feel separated from one another after the death of the father. Conflict arises out of the rights and shares of different types of property left behind by their father. But, on the whole, Bhoksa elder brothers are respected by the younger ones and his advice is sought for in almost all socio-economic and religious affairs of the family.

Sister and sister

Intimacy exists between two sisters from their childhood days till marriage comes in between them. They are always co-operative to each other, and visit each other house, thereby keeping a close relationship between the families. Generally, elder sister is the guide to her younger sister in the affairs of puberty life.

Brother and sister

They are very intimate. They are always cooperative to each other and play together, roam together and help each other in every domestic affairs. After the marriage of sister, the brothers try to keep touch with sisters. They visit sister's house. If any conflict arises between his sister and his brother-in-law, then they interfere and try to have mutual adjustment with each. If father is not alive, the divorced sister sometimes live with her brother. Brother takes responsibility for remarriage. If his sister is not married during the lifetime of the father, the brother maintains her and puts her away into marriage. It is often seen that a brother maintained his widowed sister. Brother plays an important role during the marriage of sister's son or daughter.

Grand-parent and grand-children

This relationship is very sweet and affectionate and also joking relationship exists between them and a grandfather becomes playmate to his grand son or a grand daughter. Generally, grand-father or grand-mother narrates stories to his or her grand son or daughers taking them on the lap.

Parents-in-law and daughter-in-law

When a daughter-in-law comes to the house of her parents-in-law after marriage, she then touching their feet and seek their blessings. The tender feelings and affection grow between the new bride and her husbands parents as soon as the *Gati-achar* in over after marriage. In the house of her husband, she tries to relieve her mother-in-law in every domestic affair and also her father-in-law in the field by doing different tit-bits, such as, weeding, harvesting, etc., so as to win their affection. The mother-in-law instruct her how to adapt herself to this family environment, how to carry on domestic duties smoothy, how to behave properly with relatives, how to serve the husband and other elder members of the family.

She looks after huband's parents when they fall ill. The daughter-in-law looks to her parents-in-law as her own parents and the parents of her husband also treat her as their daughter.

Attitude towards the relatives

Bhoksa are conscious about their own community. They have also fellow-feeling towards the community members. They say that a member of the community should be treated like a brother when they come in contact with any of their community members. Bhoksas address their members in the name of Ram, i.e., 'Ram Ram Saheb'. But, if any community member comes to the house of another community members, then he gives place to sit to him and enquiries about the place of his living and why he had come to visit there. If he requires help, they would cooperate with him and necessary arrangements are made for him. They are allowed to take food from their house. But when a member of the same 'gotras' of the other village come to visit the house of other community members they give him a separate place to sit. As being a member of the same gotra, he is termed as Goti-brother. Some sub-group members of the same behave each other like brothers and sisters. They wish each other and enquire about his family member, health, etc. A sub-group member is allowed to sit on chouki (a place in kitchen) and is allowed to have a smoke from the same 'hookka' and also is allowed to share food from the same plate. If he is previously unknown, then he is warmly accepted by the sub-group members. Behavioural pattern of children towards the children of the same 'gotras' of the same village or of other villages is as a friend or friends. So, when the villager of the same community, but of other sub-group comes, then they behave like friends. As they live in the same village, relation is more cordial. All the persons of the village are the neighbours and also relatives than those of their consanguineal kins and affineal kins. Among the Bhoksa non-realtives are those who are not their consanguineal or affineal unit.

Prevalence of marriage among these groups are in vogue without considering their economic status.

The Bhoksa communities have their fellow feelings towards the members, without considering villages they live in or outside their own. At the same time, sub-group consciousness is also present among them. They consider sub-group affiliation more close when any conflict arises within two groups, but at the same time, a village is considered a unit of their fellow group. There is certain good feelings about the village and its local people, who are considered almost exclusively as the villagers without regard to sub-groups, castes and cliques. They have their common attitude on many subjects. This common attitude and understanding among the members of the same village help the villagers to live together. Because at every moment they depend on others for their day-to-day life, they have their social relations as binding on their social customs. Children of the same age behave as friends. But female children sometimes maintain separate attitude towards the young boys of the other sub-group, because there is the scope of love affairs growing among the young boys and girls. Otherwise, the girls deem other boys as their brothers. In case of villagers of other castes or community, male members of a village behave friendly to each other as being a village member. Sometimes, some of them are close friends also. They are so close that they are deemed to be of their consanguineal affinal relatives, even from the members of the same group. But with others they maintain customary obligations. They are not allowed to enter into the kitchen or cannot smoke without removing *'Nigali'* (a hollo pipe made of wooden piece) which is used for ...... the children. They keep some distance from each other when an outsider comes to their house. They give a seat to sit and enquire of the reason of his coming. But female members never entertain any outsider. In case of an outsider, even if he is from the same gotra, they do not allow him to take children without removing the *Nighal.* They are not allowed to share the same cigarette and sometimes the 'Chulli'of the kitchen. At first, their attitude towards the outsider is not appreciable. But when friendship is established, they are good friends. They would help each other to the best of their ability.

Bhoksa society does not practice social hierarchy. In their view all the Bhoksas bear the same status.

Chapter - Six

LIFE-CYCLE

I

Bhoksa life-cycle is marked by the different types of rites, rituals, restrictions, prohibitions etc. After long isolation, they have come into contact with the neighbouring people and their traditional culture has been influenced by the latter. A good deal of changes have taken place in their beliefs and practices due to interaction with other groups of people. This change is more marked among the Bhoksa of Dehradun district than those of the Bhoksa of Nainital.

In this chapter, different phases of Bhoksa life-cycle have been dealt with in order to show how an individual passes from one phase of life to another, and how the society makes him equipped to adjust himself with the different phases of life.

II

Among the Bhoksa, there is no special festival either for the boys or girls to observe the puberty rite. The physical as well as mental change remind them of the appearance of puberty in them. The Bhoksas practice pre-puberty marriage. Sometimes a boy is put into marriage even at the age of 10 with a girl of 7 years. Both the parties send their *Bira*, a necessary thing for contract of marriage. The boy or girl has to perform some ritual rites for the contract of marriage. This has some influence in the life of boys and girls which help them grow a feeling about married life. Actually among the females, the age of first menstruation is treated as puberty age. As females are married at an early age, so the young women are made aware about the fact by the elder women that every female possess a monthly blood circulation course, i.e., *Mahawry*.

Pregnancy is determined by them by the absence of monthly course. If the women does not menstruate at the fix date or day in a month, then it is thought that the woman is pregnant. But the continuous missing of three menstruation periods make them sure that the female is pregnant. Generally, Bhoksa count the months of pregnancy from the day of stopping of the menstruation. The midwives of the village Tiparpur of Dehradun district say that pregnancy is counted from the date of stopping of menstruation, but at the same time they follow the different phases of moon. If menstruation stops at the full moon, then they count from the 1st day of the brighter part of the moon. A Bhoksa midwife of Pipal Sanna village of Nainital district says that the date of last menstruation is the actual date of counting the pregnancy of a woman. Full-moon denotes end of the month.

Determining of sex is a very difficult job. They have their own conception about the determination of sex. In Dehradun district, Bhoksas believe that if the women delivers in the 9th month of her pregnancy, then this will be a son; if later, then this will be a girl. But the midwife and some Bhabaras determine sex of a baby by the position of the foetus, if the foetus is placed centrally or on the right side then this may be a son; if placing of the foetus is on the left side, then this may be a girl.

There is no traditional ritual for observing the birth rites prevalent in their coustoms. And also have no restrictions or taboos and rituals found in connection with pregnancy. Women are generally free from every kind of prejudices. The only instruction is there that she should be conscious about her health. If she feels uneasy, then she should take rest. Generally, it is found, that pregnant women also go into jungle for carrying firewood. Working in the field, cooking in the house, fetching water and participating in other household activities are not forbidden. In the advanced stage of pregnancy, that is, actually from 7th to 10th months, the other members of the family, specially the elderly women of the family always keep watch on her condition. But, they give emphasis on hard labour within the household premises, but she is not allowed to carry heavy weight. They are of the view, that working is good for health of a pregnant women. They won't allow a pregnant woman of the advanced stage to go into the jungle and work in the field. During pregnancy, she usually is provided with good food, such as, 'papaya fruit', 'Makki ka roti', 'Dal', (mainly *Urdi ka dal*) etc., that is, food which contain enough protein, fat etc.

It is a custom among the Bhoksa of Dehradun district that children should be born in their father's house. They won't allow a women to deliver in her parent's place. Birth usually takes place within the four walls of the dwelling house. A dry and protected portion of the house is selected as the place of delivery. But in Nainital district, the first issue should be in the girl's house. They think that girls will be kept more comfortably in her father's house where she has friends and relatives to whom she is free in all respects. She can get assistance and help from them and her mother. It is found that the child who is born in its maternal uncle's place, his or her name should begin with 'N' which symbolises the place of birth, that, is 'Nannsare' i.e., his or her maternal grand-father's house.

Bhoksas are reputed for sorcery. So, there are magical rites prevalent in connection with the child birth. If a women is in trouble with her delivery, or before delivery, then they believe that some mischivious spirits have done something wrong with that women. So, they use different kinds of measures as advised by the *Bharara* to protect her from the danger. Sometimes, they use amulet given by *Bharara* and perform some magical rites as instructed by the *Bharara*.

The birth of a child generally takes place in a separate room of the house. Among the Bhoksa community, there are midwives, in every village. They are called at the time of delivery of a child. The midwife or *Dhai* is a local woman who is well reputed in dealing with the case of delivery. When a woman gets labour pain, then she is called in. She attends to the patient with other elderly woman. She observes the patient's condition and do the needful. Generally, household members pray to their god or goddesses for a safe delivery and welfare of both the mother and the baby. No male member is allowed to enter into the delivery room. Females ill-reputed as witches are also prohibited from entering into the delivery room. Generally, the *Dhai* gives *Sajayan* juice before the delivery to the expectant mother, which is prepared by *Noan-Water-Alachi-tea* leaves and jaggery. This is prepared without milk. They think that this would help in quick delivery. According to some *Dhais,* their general procedure of delivery is the kneeling methods. But if the case is serious, then they first advice the expectatnt mother to lie straight on ground, as straight as she can. Then they tell her to stand erect and then to kneel down. This process helps a safe delivery of an expectant mother. One of the old Bhoksa *Dhai* of Dheradun district says that in this process easy delivery can be ensured, if there is no other influence in the patient's body, such as, effects of spirits or ghosts. After delivery, the *Dhai* cuts the umbilical cord with the help of a blade or sometimes with a knife. The placenta is burried in the ground outside the compound by the *Dhai*. It is their belief that if any animal eats this placenta, then this will affect the mother badly. After the birth of a child, the Dhai again gives the mother *Sajaon* juice, which makes her body hot and help proper ejection of the after-birth matters that may create diseases. The *Dhai* is fully responsible for the conditions of the mother and the baby. After the birth of a child, the mother and the baby are cleaned with hot water by the *Dhai*. Mother is given food made with ghee (clarified butter). Rice is restricted for the mother.

The period of pollution is for 10 days. This pollution is observed for all the members of the family. On the sixth day, both the mother and the child are bathed by the *Dhai*. Females of the village sing songs for the welfare of the child. But the actual festive day is the 10th day or the day of 'Bari Puja' or 'Hoi devi puja'. In this 'puja' females take an active part. They sing songs in the name of Hoi devi. Sometimes, family members arrange for a feast. From this day the mother is allowed to do family works. Generally, on this day family members give 10 kg. *Anag* (Rice or white Dal) to the Dhai as her remuneration for the service. Ordinarily, one Bhoksa baby sucks her mother's breast upto 2 to 3 years. No other milk is used by them. In some exceptional case, they perfer to give the baby, cow milk.

III

Marriage ceremony consists of a number of phases (parts), the first and the foremost being negotiation between two parties. The *sagai* or *magni* (betrothal) comes next. Thirdly, the tentative date of marriage is fixed by the bride's family members and relatives and the same is informed to the family of bride-groom for the festival of Tika. The 'Tika', which consists of one coconut, turmeric powder, rice and oil is made by the the pandit, on the forehead of the boy and that day the Pandit declares the date of marriage by studying the pair astrologically. He also mentions about the difficulties which may arise during the conjugal life of the would-be couple. These difficulties are locally called *Ban.* Pandit, i.e., a scholar reads the letter, inform the villagers and declares the date of marriage. *Ganana* is a ceremony of fixing date of marriage. The representative of the bride-groom comes to the bride's house with the Brahmin and the *Nai,* (barber) The Brahmin fixes the date of marriage.

To remove the bad effects of the stars, which the Pandit might find on bride and bride-groom, it is to be nutralised by smearing with a paste of turmeric in oil on the body of the bride and the groom. This paste is applied on the body either of the bride or the groom-as many times as possible, according to the declaration of the Pandit. He wears new cloths which are presented to him by his father. A big piece of *Gur* is placed in front of the tray on a plate. 'Rajai' is worn by the boy. According to their view, on the day of *sagai,* the groom is the supreme person, as a king. So, he is made to sit at a more elevated place than others. All the villagers who come to attend this festival, present Rs.1/- or Rs. 2/- each as a token of good wish; Bira, which is sent by the girl's father, is opened in front of the villagers.

IV

i) Magni : (betrothal). It is a ceremony by which marriage negotiation is finalised. Some sort of understanding is brought between the two parties (families) through intermediaries of the respected villagers. In this ceremony, the boy's father presents his would-be daughter-in-law with Re.1/- which means the finalisation of marriage. 'Sagai ' is done and afterwards the girl's father is to send *Bira* to the selected boy. The boy's father has the obligation now to announce the selection of the girl as his daughter-in-law socially, and accept the *Bira* sent by the father of the girl. *Bira* represents the considered as *ashirbad,* i.e., blessing of the girl's parents towards their would-be son-in-law. This ceremony of accepting *Bira* by the boy is called *Sagai. Sagai* festival is popular among the Bhoksas. In this festival, the boy's father invites his relatives and villagers, Brahmin (priest) and *Nai* (barber) also in this festival. Villagers and relatives are invited to attend the *Sagai* festival. The boy, whose *Sagai* is arranged, is supposed to sit on a small wooden chouki. He wears new cloths which are presented to him by his father. A big piece of *Gur* (coarse sugar) is placed in front of on a tray. A Rajai (cotton swal) is worn by the boy. According to their view, on the day of *Sagai,* the groom is the supreme person. So, he is made to sit at a more elavated place than other assembled guests.

Villagers and relatives present Re.1/- or Rs. 2/ - each as a token of good wish. *Bira,* which is sent by the girl's father, is opened in front of the villagers. *Bira* contains- a new piece of cloth, Re.1/

- turmeric, 'durb-grass' and charcoal. A coin of one rupee represents good fortune, *haldi* or turmeric is to represent good health, the durb-grass is to represent prosperity and long life, the charocal is to remind them of death and to impress upon them the necessity of leading a good life, (Census 1931). After the 'Nai', i.e. barber opens the *Bira* the 'tika' ceremony starts. The Nai makes a tika on the forehead of the boy with turmeric powder from the bira plate. Then the Nai pierces the big piece (coarse sugar candy-Gur) of *Gur* by an iron rod. Women of the village sing songs for the welfare of the boy. Generally, on the occasion of *Sagai*, villagers arrange for chorus songs for entertainment. A feast is also arranged by the groom's father. The *Sagai* means finalization of contract of marriage for their respective parties.

V

In case of the Bhoksas of Dehradun district, when some sort of understanding is brought about between the two families about marriage, then the father of the boy presents Re.1/- to the girl. After some days the father of the girl visits, with other relatives, the bridegroom's house and presents Re.1/- to the boy. Villagers and other relatives of the bridegroom are invited in this 'Tika' ceremony. The actual ceremony of marriage consists of four stages, that is, Mandao, Tel-ki-roti, Ratiaya, and barat. Among the Bhoksas of Nainital district, wedding feast is an important part of their marriage ceremony. And this festival of 'Ratjaga' starts three days before the actual marriage ceremony.

'Ratjaga' is a social ceremony. The cremony begins three days before the actual marriage day. Ratjaga ceremony starts by giving *Pind* to the fore-fathers. The women of the village accompanied with the mother of the groom/bride or brother-in-law go on singing all the night. If the groom is the eldest son of his father, then the other relatives are also permitted to accompany the mother. They husk out rice by using their traditional husking device. This rice is used for offering *Pind* to their deceased fore-fathers. Father of the boy first cooks rice and mixes the rice with *ghee* (i.e., clarified butter) and then prepares *Pind* with that rice. The father of the boy then put a *Pind* in the name of his deceased father first, next a 'Pind' is put in the name of his deceased grandfather. In this way, he puts as much 'Pind' as is possible in the name of deceased forefahters. He puts these 'Pind' on the ground. These 'Pinds-giving ceremony is called as *gotrachar*. After gotrachar is completed, the female members of the village assemble in the house of the boy. They spend the whole night by singing songs. Then the help of the Pandit is sought to fix the date of marriage. Actual marriage ceremony consists of four parts :-

i) Mandao

ii) Telka Roti,

iii) Ban, and

iv) Barat-ka-Roti.

The second day of marriage is termed as Mandao. This festival is done in both the girl's and boy's houses. Actually, this is meant for removing the *Ban* to appease the unfavourable star. The Sister-in-law applies *Ban* on the body of the boy. If the son is the eldest one, then Nai (Barber) takes this *Ban* job. She gets Re.1/- for her work and there is a feast for the villagers and also for relatives. This feast is termed as *Tel-ka-Roti.* On the evening of Mandao day, there is *Vat* (Token from the relatives) which have some social significance. *Vat* is given by the close relatives, such as, maternal uncle, or uncles. Maternal uncle, or sons of maternal uncle, comes to the bride's or bridegroom's house with rice, dal, flour, ghee etc. If the *Vat* does not come from the house of the maternal uncle, then the family members of the family of the maternal uncle will never be able to take rice or roti from the house of the niece. If the body has no maternal uncle then the mother's sister has the right to give the *Vat*. In the *Vat* ceremony, the villagers and other relatives give Re.1/- to Rs. 10/- according to their capacity, as a token of love and gratitude or as a social obligation towards the festival of Mandao. This money is spent for the marriage festival. The third day is termed as *Barat-ka-din*. The men who are willing to go with the bridegroom, will come to the house of the bridegroom. There is a feast termed as *Barat-ka-roti*. On this day, the Nai removes 'Tel' and Haldi' from the body of the bridegroom and gives a bath to him. On the other hand, similar festival is there in the bride's house where the bride is given a bath by the wife of the Nai. Nai gets Rs.5/- or Rs.7/- from the bridegroom for the services. Similar is the case in the bride's house, the wife of their *Nai* gets some amount for her services. After bath the groom puts on his marriage dress and is ready to start for *Barat* (Bridegroom Procession). Similarly, in bride's house the bride is also dressed into the bridal robes after a bath.

VI

After dressing, the bridegroom goes to worship *Khera* godess and also to worship Vimsen, riding on the back of *Jija* (sister-in-law). And then the *Barat* is ready to go to bride's house. When the *Barat* reaches near the house of the bride, then the relatives of the bride, make a temporary shelter for the *Barat* party. This temporary shelter is termed as *Jalmasa.* No *Barat* party is permitted to enter the bride's house directly. The Barat party stays in the *Jalmasa* and they send message to the bride's father to the effect that Barat has reached the *Jalmasa.*

Then a person who is the representative of the bride's party, comes with *Pandit* and the *Nai.* Particularly, the bride's brother will come with the Nai (barbar) and the *Pandit* (priest). If the bride has no brother, then a person, who is in the category of bride's brother comes. The *Pandit* comes with some materials, such as, turmeric 'choul', 'deep' and Re.1/-, then the bride's brother touches the feet of the bridegroom and offers Re.1/- and the Pandit chants mantras. This is called *Panchak.* After *Panchak, Barat* is permitted to enter into the bride's house. There is a custom of firing from a gun or display of fire-works to symbolize a Rajput marriage. At the entrance of the bride's house, *Dooar Bar* (stoppage at the door) is held. In *Dooar Bar,* the bridegroom is surrounded by Jija and other friends. This is the time of joking between these two parties, i.e., the Barat party and the bride's party. This time bride's party serves tea and snacks for the bridegroom's party. After taking tea, the bridegroom's party returns to *Jalmasa.* They again come to bride's house for feast. That time, the bridegroom takes rice with some leafy vegetables under the *chai* this is called *sagvati* (rice and vegetables). After completing *Barat-ki-roti* and *Sagvati* or bridegroom, they again return to *Jalmasa.* At the dead of night when the *lagan* is there, the bride's party comes to *Jalmasa* and take bridegroom with *Jija* to *chai* and then the actual marriage takes place. Then *vamar* or circumbulation is done, first four times by the bride and then three times by the bridegroom.

VII

Next day of the marriage, there is *Bidai* (Culmination of the marriage and saying good bye). In this festival, the bride touches the feet of her relatives, relatives present money to the bride, according to their capacity. This money is for the pocket expenses of the bride during journey. After that *Barat* returns to the bridegroom's house. The traditional transport of bride and bridegroom is the *Dholi*. But at present they have changed it. Sometimes bride and bridegroom return by taxi, or by bus or by tractors. In the Nainital district, at the wedding post a cut piece of *Semul* tree is fixed in front of the house of each party and over that a Mondop is arranged (small improvised pandal). In the Dehradun district, only a pandal is erected for marriage ceremony itself. But in Nainital district, *Chai* (Bom becaceae tree for platform) ceremony has some social significance. For cutting *Chai* the bridegroom's elder sister's husband or younger sister's husband is the socially recognised person. If the bridegroom has no such relatives, then a relative of the same category of the lineage who has the joking relation with the bridegroom can be permitted to cut the 'Chai' or fix the 'Chai' in front of the house. For cutting and collecting Chai is a troublesome matter for some persons, because their social customs do not permit them to cut the *Chai*. The *Jija* (Elder sister's husband) of the bridegroom, who takes the responsibility for cutting and putting *Chai* in front of the house, can be intervened by the other members of the bridegroom's categories; as such, they can harass him by using their urine to Chai, when he is going to cut it.

When 'Jija' goes to cut a Chai or a Semul tree, he should take seven konkon (this konkon is made of pind,) which is made up of (Salt, haldi, lang,

Durbagrass for the protection of the bridegroom from the effects of spirits and ghosts). When he cuts the Semul tree (......) for the purpose of *Chai,* and the stem of the 'Semul' tree, he will be selected for the *patila* or sitting place for the bridegroom or bride when *haldi* or Ban will be given to the bride or the bridegroom. For the worship of the *Chai,* Jija will take Puri, Chawal, Dal and Haldi in two *Datai.* After cutting the Semul (......) tree, Jija will put 10 paisa at the stem of the tree as the cost of the tree to *Datri mata* (the goddess of the earth). Then *Jija* worships this Chai on putting a *konkon* at his hand, one is tied on the *Chai,* another one is tied with *Kulhari* and the others are carried by him. One is for the brother-in-law of the bridegroom. And out of the remaining two, one is for the bridegroom and the other is for the bride. After Chai puja, Jija of the bride or bridegroom returns to village with *Chai, patili* and some of the bound grass and put the same in front of the house. When the Jija is going to put the *Semul tree* or *Chai* on the mandap Jija, with his strength, puts the Chai on the mandap, all the female members with whom he has the joking relationship, throw water on him. Sometimes water mixed with cowdung and termeric etc. are also thrown on him from his attempt to stop the Chai, then Jija puts the Chai in front of the Verandah and then tie some grass on the Chai. Actually, Chai is the identification of a marriage festival in the house. On the next day of marriage, very early in the morning, sisters, and brothers-in-law of the bridegroom dance on the roof of the house as they believe that this will do good for the newly married couple. They pray to god for blessing on the newly married couple to save them from the spirits and ghosts. When the Barat party returns with the newly weds, they are made to stay in front of the Chai (a stem of tree). Then the game of fish catching is arranged in front of the 'Chai'. This game is meant to entertain the new bride and through this game the new bride is introduced to the young people of the house and the villagers as well. A pond-like hole is dug and the bridegroom hides something, may-be some coin into that hole. The bride is to find it out. The sisters of the bridegroom and his brothers-in-law help the bride to search the thing out from this small pond. This is done for seven times. Then the bride hides something into the pond. Now it is the turn of the bridegroom to search it out. Jija or elder sister's husband, and friends can help the bridegroom to find it out. In this way, they entertain the bride and bridegroom. After the game, the new bride distributes some Puri and Halua which she brings from her father's house to her mother-in-law's house.

At night, there is the ceremony of Gotratantar. Groom's father takes active part in the ceremony of changing Gotra of the bride. Both bridegroom and bride sit together at a place. The father of the bridegroom puts some *Pind* (funeral cake) in the hand of his son and then the son gives it to his wife. And the wife puts the Pind on ground in the name of the forefathers of the bridegroom. After completing *Gotratantar.* The bride is treated as a members of the bridegroom's *gotra*. Thus, the post marital festival comes to an end. But on the third day after marriage, a group of persons come to the bridegroom's house from the bride's house. This is called *Dasora.* This time the bridegroom gives a feast to them, and the girl returns to her father's house. There, she distributes *Puri* and *Halua* to her father's villagers and relatives which she carries from the father-in-law's house. After that, on a full moon day of either in the month of Magh, or Falgun, she comes back to her father-in-law's house permanently. This return of her to her father-in-law's house is called *Choula.*

VIII

Bhoksas classify death in two parts i.e., natural death (Kal) and un-natural death (Bakal). The former is again divided into six types, and later they are divided into 36 types. When a person dies after completing his satisfaction of life, i.e., having sons, daughters and without suffering from any diseases or not due to any kind of bad events, is called a natural death. Death due to some accident or by suffering from diseases etc. is called un-natural death. Actually the man who dies without having completed his worldly satisfaction or is unmarried, or married having no child, is termed as an un-natural (Bakal) death and is bad for the society and people of the community or villagers.

In case of death, their concept is related to the doctrine of work. The man who works for the benefit of the people never dies a *Bakal* or un-natural death. They also believe that there is certain power, i.e., God who writes the fate of a person and that is final, that cannot be changed by any means. Six kinds of 'Kal'-deaths are there, e.g., (1) a man who died after completing wordly satisfaction, (2) a man who dies having sons and daughters, (3) a man who dies suffering from any kind of diseas, (4) a man who dies without falling from tree, (5) a man who does not die of or due to snake bite or not as a prey to a tiger and (6) the man who does not die due to evil eye.

They are able to tell only about 14 kinds out of the thirty-six cases of Bakal deaths. These are as follows :

(1) In child-hood age, (2) Without having children, (3) Unmarried, with sons, (4) Influence of evil eye,

(5) Influence of ghost, (6) Influence of Bhutni, (7) Influence of witch-craft, (8) Anger of gods and goddesses, (9) Fall from the tree, (10) Death by drowning, (11) Death in forest, (12) Death in open field, (13) Murdered by others, (14) Death due to an attack by tiger or by other wild animals, (15) Death due to snake bite, (16) Death due to heavy rain, (17) Death in ice, (18) Death due to thunder storm, (19) Death due to accident etc. Other untimely deaths are considered to have occurred under head Bakal death.

Death and Funeral

When a person either male or female dies, the women and the children of the family lament loudly by the side of the deceased. If death occurs at night, then the family members wait till dawn for funeral. There should be some male person in the house, where death has occurred, to observe the funeral rites. Generally, all the villagers are informed of the death. In Dehradun district, the villagers are informed of the death of any co-villagers by the *Bhangi*. But in Nainital district, a person from the village informs of a death in the village to all the villagers and all the relatives of the deceased. For the the relatives, living in distant villages, information is sent either through a co-villager or relatives. The villagers of the deceased's village and the relatives and friends come to console the family members. The elderly family members do not take food on the day of death. Generally, the dead-body is cleaned with water, sometimes they use hot water and in some special cases they use soap and also put some scents on the dead-body for removing the bad smell. The dead-body is generally washed by his or her sons or daughters, but if he or she had no issue, then in the case of a male his wife will clean it, and in the case of a female, a female relative of the deceased female will do the washing of the body. Then the dead-body will be covered with a white cloth.

In Dehradun district, when information of death is received by a person, then it is his duty to attend the funeral procession or to send one person from his house for attending the funeral procession with some fuel wood for burning the dead-body. Thus, the people of the village or of the neighbouring villages assemble at a place with fire wood. This wood is used for the cremation of the dead-body. But the Bhoksas of Nainital do not carry wood from their house for burning. They collect dry wood from the jungle. All the Bhoksa cremation of Nainital district are is deep forests where flows a stream.

Danaza (needed for funeral) is a ladder-like structure. Danaza is made by the villagers and relatives of the deceased. This is prepared by putting two large wooden beams longitudinally and 11 small wooden sticks for carrying a short statured dead-body, and for tall statured body, horizontally tied to the longitudinal beams with rope. After making the structure of the Danaza, they put some grass on it and sometimes they use bed of the deceased person on it. Before placing the dead-body of a male on the Danaza, his wife should break her *Churi* (glass bangles) of her hands and should put off ornaments of her hands and ornaments of her body, mainly the nose-pin or nose-rings which symbolise a married women. She should worship her husband's feet. Villagers would say in front of the deceased's mouth that-

"Ved hay to pran hay
Ayr dadha to Maya hai
Ya Maya Karchaha
Ved ma Vi Nahi."

Then place the dead-body on Danaza and cover it completely with a new cloth.

The cremation ground is generally situated at a distance from the village. In the village Tiparpur of Dehradun district, the cremation ground is situated on the northern side of the village on the bank of the Assam river. There is no fixed place as such for cremation. They can use any place on the bank of the Assam river according to their convenience. Generally, Dheradun Bhoksa prepare the pyre by digging the soil in a rectangular shape and then place the wood on it. The size of the pyre is made to fit a lying human body and generally it is 5' to 5 and half feet in length and 3' width and the depth is made to be 3'. When the body is placed on the pyre, it is to take into consideration that the head of the dead-body is placed in the eastern direction. The eldest son makes four rounds by the pyre and put fire on it. After completion of the burning they put long wooden poles, which are placed longitudially for preparing Danaza, into water and sprinkle the water on the pyre. This water is given by the eldest son or sons of deceased person. After sprinkling of water on the pyre, they return home.

But the Bhoksas of Nainital district do not dig the ground for cremation. They place wood in such a manner that a body can easily be placed on it. After preparation of the pyre, all the relatives and persons of the same 'gotra' put fire-wood on the pyre. Each and every relative make a bundle of dry wood and place it on the pyre with his heartist good wishes for the deceased's soul. Then they set fire to the pyre. When the pyre is blaze and they find it burning alright, they return to their own homes. After burning of the body, all of them take bath and directly go to the house of the deceased person. They smoke there and return to their homes. After three days, the villagers who participate in the funeral procession from the houses again go to the spot of cremation. They take ghee (clarified butter), fire-wood, mustered seeds and Nichilar (sacred thread). At first, they clean the spot of the cremation using water from the nearest sources. And then they draw a cordon all round the cremation spot by using the fire-wood, mustered seeds and other things, which they carried alongwith them from the house of the dead person. This is done to prevent the soul or the spirit of the deceased person to go back to his house. They spread some mustered seeds on the cremation spot, and return home. They stand in a line. Then a boy or girl of the deceased's house circumbulate round the party with a jug of water in hand. There is a belief found prevalent among them that the soul of the deceased remains on the shoulder of the men who carry the Danaza of the deceased person. It is also believed that it will remain on their shoulder till the date it is removed by the members of the deceased's family. On the third day, sons-in-law or Jija of the deceased or some other affinal relatives will purchase fish from the market and put those into fire. They carry the smell of the fish pronouching *Kanditarini Utar Jao*. This is the occassion of removing *Kanditarini*.

The period of polution varies between 10 to 13 days, according to age, 10 days polution is observed in the case of 10-year old children and 12 days for the young persons. But for the married persons it is 13 days. After disposal of the deadbody the house is cleared with cowdung. Polution is observed by all the family members and close relatives. On the 13th day, they observe the Shradh ceremony. They call a pandit for the ceremony. The Pandit offers 'Pinda' and observes havan into the room. That day, a feast is given by the family members. But the family members do not participate in this feast. They prepare rice separately which is taken by the family members and 'gotra' brothers who observe population. They prepare food separately for the guest. Those who are economically well off, engage a Brahmin cook for the preparation of food, otherwise, villagers prepare food. This feast is a simple one. The items of feast are only Rice and Dal.

They collect some bones of the deceased which generally they carry to Hardwar and there observe bone-immersion ceremony with the help of a Panda (helper). Bhoksas believe in rebirth. They have their indigenous procedure to prove re-birth of a person. Generally, on the day of disposal of the dead-body, they clean the place where the dead body is kept and make a heap of it and set fire to it. This cow-dung is kept for six days and then set on fire. Then they collect the ashes of the cow-dung in a basket and keep it in a safe place in the name of the deceased person. The mark which is found on the ashes of cow-dung is supposed to be the future life of the deceased.

Chapter - Seven

MAGICO-RELIGIOUS BELIEFS AND PRACTICES

I

To describe the major religious traditions of the Bhoksa community, it will be necessary to remember that religious traditions of the Bhoksas were the gradual blending of the pre-Brahamanical and Brahmanical norms and practices. Traditional religious concepts of the Bhoksas of the two districts are based on the existence of ghosts, demons and spirits whom they either respect or are afraid of. The prevailing religious beliefs of both the districts are a kind of Hinduism. But, it is difficult to give a definite idea about the religious beliefs of the Bhoksa community as to what the real living beliefs of the Bhoksas are. After examining the forms and the ceremonies observed by them in their daily life-both domestic and sacramental-it is found that Siva and Vishnu and their female forms are the principal objects of worship on the one hand and the polyacmonistic cult of the older tribe, on the other. Their beliefs in demons or superhuman spirits are also found, to which the term animism is now applied. Animism implies to a belief in the existence of spirits, some of whom are good to mankind and some are bad and powerful enough to compel attention through fear of their influence. They are capable of wondering anywhere they like but cannot be represented by idols, or cannot reside in some object or body living as wifeless and thus the object then becomes a felish endowed with power to protect the worshiper.

II

Bhoksas are well reputed in sorcery. Bhoksa religion is dominated by magico-religious beliefs. They believe in super-human power. They have numerous deities and spirits in the village and family pantheon. "They had great reverence for the Muslim saints and Sikh Guru and other religious Gurus of different sects, including all statutory ways of dealing with super-normal powers and magic which cover all bad ways of dealing with them"- this is quite applicable to Bhoksa society also. Their social life is much influenced by magic-a belief in supernatural. To perform the magico-religious activities, there are several religious functionaries specialities among the Bhoksa. Their views in a village Council among the community members is considered very weighty, especially in matters for deciding the cases referred to it. They are :

i) Guru or Jogi.

ii) Sidh or pir.

iii) Podhan (khum-podhan)

iv) Bhagat and

v) Bharara.

The Gurus are the religious specialists of difference sects. The main section of Bhoksa Guru's are Nathjogies, who visit the Bhoksa are once in the year and make them desciples of Natha sect. Some

Gurus of Ramayat sect also visit the Bhoksa area occasionally. Bhoksas respect Guru as their guide in religious matters. They worship gods or goddesses under his guidance and recite the hymes, which Guru teaches them. The voice of the Guru is always accepted by the members of the Bhoksa community. As they believe in the words that obeying of Gurus orders and fulfilment of Guru's desire is the only path to attain salvation, and after death they will thus attain the land of the heighest glory. Sidh or Pir, (Hindu and Muslim saint who acquires supernatural power in his possession, able to cure disease or able to do some supernatural deeds) is respected by the Bhoksa. They visit the Ashram of Sidh or Masjid of Pir with some problems, both personal and of family. In Nainital, Mani Ram Singh is very popular among them. Although Sidh Mani Ram died many years ago, yet his place of worship is respected by the Bhoksa members of Nainital. As such, in Dheradun they also respect Sidh.

Generally, worship of the Khera or Chandi in Nainital and also Bhumia of Dehradun are held twice a year. This is held after harvest. In the Nainital district, the village head or Khum-podhan has the right to worship the Khera God & Goddess thus prodhan is not available, then any of the male member of the Podhan's family can worship the Khera goddess. But in Dehradun district, only a Brahmin has the right to worship the god or goddess of Bhumia.

III

Khera is the village as well as the community god of the Bhoksa of Nainital district, whereas Bhumia or Khera is worshipped by the Bhoksa of Dehradun District as a village god only. In Nainital district, in every village there is a *Than of Chandi or Khera* for worship. The place of worship of Chandi or Khera god is generally situated at the outskirt of the village and normally near the river-side or under the Bel-tree (wood apple tree) or the Pipal-tree. The *Than* is an alter made of mud of the measurement of 5′ x 6′ size, with an elevation of 1/2′. On the said alter, there exists seven elevations. The alter with all the seven elevations in a body is termed as Khero or *Chandi-ka-Than*. The middle one, which is the largest in size and highest in elevation than the others, is known as Chandi. Other mounds are subordinates to the goddess Chandi who help the goddess to maintain her power. The moud on the right hand side of the goddess Chandi represents Purbia which is the first, then Trishmarkha is the second and Nathuram is the third. They were prominent Bhoksa Bhararay (sorcerers) of the past. The heaps on the left hand side are Dhano which is the first one, Bhut and spirits are the second and Maniram Sidh is the third one. The name of the heaps are different in other Bhoksa inhabited villages. Generally, a difference is found in the right hand side heaps where Bhoksa Bhararas are placed. The inclusion of Bharara in the *Than* of Chandi or Khera completely depended on the reputation of that particular Bharara and his good deed or service to the community, e.g., Purbia is included because he is the person who introduced the magic among this community.

By birth, Purbia was a Bhoksa. From his childhood he was interested in training sorcery. The myth goes that he want to Kamrupdesh of Bengal to learn magic. After learning magic from the Kamrupdesh, he returned to his own land and served his own people by sorcery. It requires mentioning here that he was the founder of sorcery among the Bhoksa community. Before Purbia there was no sorcerer among the Bhoksa. The whole of his life time he served the Bhoksa people by his magical hymes, Bhoksa people believe that he removed all the evil spirits or Bhut Dano, who are harmful to mankind from the Bhoksa inhabited villages and drove away all these evil spirits into jungle. The spirits who are in jungle or in the forest do not harm anybody if he regularly worship Purbia. Further, a badly affected family may be saved or a ruined person may get life in danger by taking the name of Purbia. It is also believed by the Bhoksa that any kind of black magic can be stopped by his name.

Tirishmar Kha was a prominent Bhoksa leader; he was actually a man from Tharu tribe, but was closely associated with the Bhoksa. He was a reputed sorcerer among the Bhoksa community. He spent most of the time of his life with the Bhoksas and served them by his magical hyms and also by traditional medicines.

Nathu Ram was a Bhoksa, he was one of the reputed sorcerer of the Bhoksa community. He deals with diseases of women, especially at the time of pregnancy and child birth. Similarly, Mana Kangar was as person of Harizon or Bhangi caste, who was reputed as a popular Bhoksa sorcerer and served all through his life time for the welfare of the Bhoksa. He also dealt with the diseases of women and children. He was reputed in the treatmet of snake bites and for some medicine of other insects bite too. So it is found that some of the villages where Manaknajar is included in the *Than* of Chandi or Khera in the place of Nathuram (instead of Nathu Ram).

Chountra or Maniram was the founder of the Pipal Sanna village. He was the Khum head, i.e., in the British period the Khum head was the liaison person between the village or community members and British Government authorities, i.e., Khum Superintendent. All the land of the village was in the name of Khum-head. And he was the responsible person to distribute lands among villages and to collect the revenue from the respective houses of the village and deposit it to the Khum authorities. Because of his traditional position, he was treated as a philosopher and guide to the people of the village. He loved villagers and gave them necessary help in times of exigency. So, it is believed by the Bhoksas that, as he was the founder of the village, and as he loved the villagers so much so that they are under the impression that even after his death he could not dissociate himself from the village. The villages Cremated the body of Mani Ram at the outskirt of the village. The place where his body was cremated is honoured with termed as *Chountra*. The Bhoksa believe that his soul always protect them from any sort of apprehended loss. Every year at the time of Holi festival, they worship the soul of the village head at *Chountra* with 'puri', 'halwa' etc. The elder members of lineage of the deceased headman mainly officiate over this worship and other villagers take part in this Pujas. But in the village Khumbari, there is no *Chountra,* 'Khumbari' was coined after the name of the place of Kum-office where office of the temporary office of the khum authorities was established. But most of the other old villages have their own *Chountra*.

It is also believed by the villagers that the soul of a founder of the village never get salvation. His soul always moves throughout the village proper. The soul always tries to do good for the villagers on the eve of any danger of the village. The soul of the village headman inspired the villagers, sometimes by appearing in dream to any persons of the village and suggests the way out from the danger. Villagers worship *Chountra* by offering 'Halua' & 'Puri' on the day of Deewali festival.

In Dehra Dun district, 'Bhumia' is the term used for village god. Khera or the place of worship of Bhumia is located generally at the outskirt of the village or at the middle of the village itself, under a peepul tree or *aswatha* tree. In the place of Khera, other gods or goddesses are also worshipped along with Bhumia, by the Bhoksa people. Bhumia is a god or goddess who actually rules over the village land. According to Bhoksa of Dehradun, the Khera or Bhumia look after the welfare of the villagers and saves them at the time of danger, if the god is pleased with the villagers. The worship of the Khera and Bhumia is a contributory one. For the worship of Khera or Chandi, prodhan of the respective villages collect an amount fixed by him from each and every household of the village. The Prodhan fixes a date of worship of Chandi and on that day everyone of the village comes to the *than* of Chandi to participate in the worship of the goddess. Prodhan performs Homan in front of the *Than* of Chandi. Nainital Bhoksa do not use any Brahmin for the worship of goddess Chandi or in Khera-pujan.

But in Dehra Dun, the Prodhan or some respected person of the village assemble in a place to have a meeting, and a group discussion is made about the contribution to the Khera or Bhumia worship and an amount is fixed in this meeting and collection is made accordingly. The Bhoksa of Dehradun engage a Brahmin for their *Khera pujan* or *Bhumiapujan.* A Brahmin fixes the date of worship and on that day all the villagers, including children and women, assemble at the place of Khera or Bhumia pujan. The Brahmin prays to Khera or

Bhumia god for the welfare of the village and villagers and puts homage to Khera god or goddess for the welfare of the families of the villagers. After the Bhumia pujan all the villagers return home and take food but before khera pujan nobody can take meal except the children.

IV

Bhum Sen is worshipped by the Bhoksa of Nainital district. In their view, Bhum-Sen is the owner of the lands. The Khera goddess Chandi is the supreme among all the gods and goddesses and Bhum-Sen has the authority to look after the land and agriculture. Bhum-Sen is found in the house of every Khum-Podhan or the village head whose forefather was the first settler of the village. The alter of Bhum-Sen is nothing but an alter of mud which is measured 3'x4' area and 2'x3' in elevation. As the Bhum-Sen is considered the owner of the lands, he is treated as a village god. It is their belief that if Bhum-Sen is pleased with them, then they will be free from the danger of attack of wild animals and they are also sure that their paddy will not be destroyed by the wild animals, like bears, elephants, etc. They will get constant good yields of paddy from their lands. Bhum-Sen also saves their village from the attack of evil spirits, ghosts, demons, etc. For the worship of Bhum-Sen they do not engage a Brahmin. Prodhan of the village is the priest of Bhum-Sen. Generally, they worship Bhum-Sen at the time of Holi festival. All the villagers prepare 'Halua', 'Puri' and 'Mitha choul' for the worship of Bhum-Sen. Prodhan of the village or any male member of his family can worship the god Bhum-Sen. Villagers gather in the home of the prodhan. They sing and dance in front of the alter of the Bhum-Sen after worship and take prosad of Bhum-

Sen on that day. They enjoy a lot. The Prodhan of the village, if he is a well-to-do man, arranges a feast for the villagers. If the Prodhan's economic condition is bad, then other members of the village jointly arrange a feast in the house of Prodhan for remembering the gracious old days of their community life.

Among the Bhoksa, Bagat is a religious man who, under the instruction of a Guru, should lead a sacred life, practical songs sacred performance became specialist termed as gagat. Generally, a Bhagat with his religiostic life is a spirit worshipper, he learnt this worship under the guidance of his Guru and can possess spirit through initiation and propitiation of a particular hymes and may treat patients with the help of spirits.

V

The Bharara, the magico-religious persons, a Bharara is a man who knows magical hymns to remove the *malevolent* effects of the spirits and have a good knowledge of local medicines. A Bharara is an ordinary man who has had to propitiate certain gods and goddesses and lead a sacred life as and when he learns the magical hymns from a Guru. A Bharara, after having gained the knowledge from a Guru, may become the Bhagat and lead a sacred life. Generally, among the Bhoksa, Bharara is recognised as a local medicine man and a spirit doctor. They treat other patients when patients visit their house or call them on any event. In this connection it requires mentioning here that some recognised Bhoksa Bharara of Nainital district are the *jajman* of the community. They get year ending food grain from the house of some community members, as retainers.

VI

It is through the rigorous training that one can master the art of becoming a Bharara. And it is for this reason, it is not open to one and all. One has to undergo training for a period of six months. During this period, one has to observe some restrictions. He should be obedient to his Guru. The trainee should obey him as his father. During the training period, he is to cook his own food and to take meal once a day. Sexual intercourse is strictly prohibited. He is not permitted to go to any relatives house and should live in a separate room and lie on the ground. Nobody, except his Guru, is permitted to enter into this room. He should wake early in the morning, take a bath and chant the mantras. If any one can undergo this sort of training under the instruction of a well reputed Bharara then he became a good Bharara. The Bhoksas say that this training is not sufficient to deal with the spirits and ghosts. If any Bharara wants to utilize the power of Spirits and Ghosts, then he should undergo further training. In this training, a trainee has to take the risk of his life. During this second spell of training, he has to go to a river and utter the mantras in addition to the aforesaid restrictions. He has to go upto neek-deep water of the river, carrying a lamp on his hands and has to continue this process for about a month or more till the respective spirits or ghosts appear to him and pledge assistance at his necessity. On successful completion of the training, he is free to lead normal life.

The Bharara describe that the magical power or skill of the Bhararas which can be used for the benefit of mankind. They say that when anybody wants to learn the art of magic from the Guru or anybody who is well aware of the magical art, he must promise to his guru that it should only be used for the protective, curative and other beneficial purposes for the people of their society. He is permitted to practice the black magic only when his life is in danger by some other Bharara. It is also said by the Bharara that if anybody uses black magic for attaining some gain or for earning money, then the family of that Bharara may be destroyed by the curse of his Guru. Magic is truth to them and hence founded on reality of life. It also acts as a means to security of their life. The Bhoksas do not think of their safety of life without the help of a Bharara. Bhararas are called by the people at every event or crisis of thier life. For instance, pregnancy, childbirth, marriage, sickness and death also for the protection of agricultural products from the attack of wild animals and to save patients from the harmful effects of the spirits and ghosts. They are called in to cure the cattle diseases also. The Bhoksa have an implicit faith in the magical power of the Bharara.

Now-a-days, it is the general view of the Bhoksa that the black magic of the Bhoksa Bharara is on the wane. But some of the Bhoksa Bharara are of the opinion that Black magic still rules the roost. Otherwise general Bhoksa people would not have recognised the art of the Bharara. This is the main secret for which the Bhararas are obeyed. If they do not keep the act of black magic secret, they will die due to the wrath of the magic gods, ghosts, spirits etc. Now, the Bhararas do not want to practice Black Magic, as the performance of Black magic requires patience and mental strength at the same time. It is also expansive. The Bhoksa Bharara of Nainital district say that ghosts and spirits like Raipapir, Kalua are the main evil spirits or ghosts who can harm to other persons. The procedure for doing Black magic by chanting Mantras of Raipa pir may be done in different ways. And the person against whom the Black magic is performed will die within a few days, suffering from liver pain, heart attack or decentery etc. Kalua is also treated as a black magic spirit. Worship of Kalua is done only for doing the black magic. The Bhoksa of Nainital district say that there are other ghosts concerning the black magic, *i.e.*, Bijlia Khera Manakanjar etc. Some of the black magic is being described later. The Bhoksa of Nainital district is also considered Narsing Mohini as black magic. It is believed by the Bhoksa that a Bharara is empowered by the mantra and can enjoy the freedom in putting a girl in his favour or to other persons whenever he desires.

Some mantras are used by the Bhoksas of both the districts. These mantras are classified into four categories, *i.e.*,

I) White magic,

II) Black magic.

III) Jocking magic and

IV) Mohini Mantras.

White magic is practiced by the Bhoksa Bharara for the welfare of the people. The Purbia, Purbba, Trishmarkha are the main spirits, and goddess Kali is the main goddess governing the white magic. When a person falls ill, the Bhoksas generally call a Bharara of their community to their house. To examine the patient, the Bharara first sees the palm of the patient and chants some mantras. They use this procedure to diognose the disease, whether the patient is affected with the spirits or by the act of the some other Bharara. If the fingers of the patient move upward, then it is assumed that the patient is a victim of spirits of ghost or other supernatural forces. If the fingers of the patient move downwards then it indicates that the patient is afflicted with some mischivious deed of other Bharara. If the fingers of the patient move both upward and downward, then it is their belief that the patient has been affected with some supernatural force, which is sent by other Bharara for causing harm to the patient. If the fingers of the patient do not move, then it is treated as a general disease.

For examining the patient, the Bharara enchants Purbia mantras for the male and for the female patient they enchant Purabba mantras. Otherwise no result will be found, because female mantras should be used for the female and the male mantras should be used for the male, in general. But in some cases, specially when the fingers of the patient move both upward and downward, then only the Bharara uses both the male and female mantras, i.e., Purbia and Purabba. This test may also be done by enchanting the mantras of Trishmarkha for the male and goddess kali for the female. The mantras of Goddess Kali can be used for both male and female. Generally, the Bharara uses different mantras depending on the condition of the patient in consideration of the Bharara to provide the benefit of the patient.

VII

Bharoo is a ghost, who helps a Bharara if his treatment. According to the Bharara, he helps keep the suprimacy of the Bharara when he works. Bharoo helps Bharara to remove supernatural spirits or ghosts from the body of the affected person when the Bharara chants his mantras on the body of the patient. It is believed by the Bhoksa that if this Bharoo is sided by a Bharara, then only this become effective. To make the *mantrasidh* Bharara chants this mantras thousand times when they are in the learning stage. The Bhoksa Bharara generally uses this mantra when anybody is affected by the super-natural spirits or ghosts. It is believed by the Bhoksa Bharara that Buro has the power to control the ghost sent by other.

VIII

Jokes also occupy a good place in there magical skill, both black and white. Jocking by magic is prevalent among the Bhoksa of both the districts. According to them, the magic for jocking is guided by *Tumri* The popular 'Tumri' among them is Tataia as well as flute. But there is danger in the way of practicing the fluite magic also. If the flutish fails to resist the entry of the fluite into his mouth, then it may entail danger for him. Generally in joking magic, the Bhararas who joke with others use its remedy after joking. these joking magic are done by the Bharara for showing his magical power to others or sometimes to punish the person who visit their area unauthorisedly and claim that he knows magic better than the Bhoksa Bharara. After jocking by magic they make a compromise, or sometimes a misbehaved flute-player begs forgiveness to the Bharara and promise not to misbehave again with the villagers or other community members. In other cases, specially in dealing with cases of small pox or to control epidemic of cholera, the Bharara must observe fast.

IX

They say that the mantras pronounced by the Bharara during any rite for bringing about some definite result have a supernatural sanction behind them. This mystic power is responsible for bringing about the desired effect. It is said that the sorcerers were capable of transforming men into animal and keep them under control. The Sorcerers were said to accomplish their nefarious purpose with the aid of some mischievous spirits. The Bhararas used to adopt the spirits as their associates and to keep them in good humour used to make sacrifices. It is also said that their power of magic and sorcery seems to have considerably waned as a result of conflict between the practitioners of the black magic. The practice of black magic has practically disappeared and white magic holds the sway now.

Purbia (Gents)

Purab sa kaoun chalu,
Purbia chalu
Kaha kaha lata chalu
Char bir lata chalu,
Ourka chauli torti chalu,
Apni chauki lagat chalu,
Mari guruki ann lagati chalu.

Purbia (Male)

Who has come from East ?
Purbia has come
Along with four Birs
He went on destroying others centre
And setting up his own centre.

Who moves from the east ? He is Purbia. What he has taken with is four Birs (a kind of ghost spirit) ? He sets his magical power breaking other men's magic there. This is in the name of his Guru. He sets his magical power.

Purbha (Ladies)

Purab sa kaoun chalu

Purbba Chalu

Kaha kaha lata chalu

Chausatt jogini chappan kalua

Bahann bir

Mari guru ki ann nanna chammari ki ann

Purbba (Female)

Who moves from the East ?

The purbba is moving.

She has with her 64 Jogines and 56 kalua,

She went on killing the bad spirits

And destroying others centres.

This is in the name of her guru and that of Nannachamari.

Who moves from the east ? She is purbba. What she takes with her is 64 jogini (a kind of ladies spirits)? 56 kalua (a kind of harmful ghost), 52 Birs (a kind of ghosts who have power of doing both good and evil). This is in the name of my Guru and also in the name of Nanna Chammari, a popular Bhoksa Bharara in this area.

Tirishmar Kha (Gents)

Uttarakhanda sa kaoun chalu

Tirishmar kha chalu

Kaha kaha la ta chalu

Hath ma Banduk la ta chalu,

Mari guru ki ann lata chalu.

Tirishmar kha (Male)

Who has come from North ?

Tirishmar kha has come,

Carrying a gun in his hand

He is moving in the name of his Guru.

Who moves from the northern region, he is Tirishmar Kha, what he takes with him. He has taken a rifle in his hand. This will become active in the name of my Guru.

Kali

Joy kong kali mahakali
Indrakabati brahmaki sali
Tarati chali baithati chali
Nann chammari ki ann

Kali (Common)

Oh Victorious konkali Mahakali
Daughter of Indra and sister-in-law of Brahma
Disobeying the other hymn and establishing
Your own place
It is your promise and of my Guru
and that woo in the name of Nannchamari.

With the best wishes of mother goddess Kali who is daughter of Indra and wife's sister of Brahma, she moves breaking the other power and to establish her power actively. This is in the name of Nann Chambari.

Ulkamaie (Ladies)

Purab sa kaoun chalu?
Ulkamalie chali,
Kaha kaha lata chali,
Chausatt jogini chappan kalua
Kahann bir la ta chali
Orki chauki torti chali

Mari ann mari guru ki ann,

Nann chamari ki ann.

Ulkamaee (Female)

Who has come from East ?

Ulkamaee has come,

She has with her

64 Joginis, 56 kaluas and 52 Birs,

On her way she destroys the camp of others

And instead setting up her own

That is in the name of Nann chammari

Who moves from the east, is I:La?AOE. wjat sje tales wotj jer os 64 Jogini (a kind of ladies spirits) 56 Kalua (a kind of harmful ghosts), 52 Birs (a kind of Ghosts who has the power of doing both good and evil. She sets her magical power to break other magic. This is in the name of herself, her guru and also in the name of Nann Chamari, a popular Bhoksa Bharara in this area.

Mohini

Til ka tali charaharali

Atika nann mayee

Jatika sishmaie

Chalaja mohini Batto Batto

Ja baithuja falanaka ghat

Rot iko manala sotiko gagala

Jal sa hill kutt ti abay

Gaye sa takrati aba

Ororka dakhka laga pajara

Mari dekhaka rang sa darry

Til oil is on the palm :

Bright as Nayanmani,

When the Til oil is on the palm dazzle like Naya,
When Til oil is on the palm
dazzle like Nayanmani,
And when evaporates it looks like Sishmayee
The Rajamayee even sits on the leaf
And Nayanmayni sits on the Piri
Oh Mohni you go in her steps
And sit in the house (name of the person concerned)
You don't allow her to eat
Awake the sleeping woman,
She will come even through the knee deep water
She will come defying the attack of cow
She will come swaying in the air
Seeing the other she will feel shy
But to see me she will smile.

The oil of 'teel' (a kind of grain) seeds in hand, two mother goddesses control it, that is Nayan maie and shishmaie. Go mohini, on her every step of foots. Go and sit in the house of that woman and do that she could not take food, she could not sleep properly, she could come into the water which sink upto her knees, if it is the stromy day she should come. If she faces the attack of cow then also she will come. She should become angry with any one except me.

Bhero

Kala bhero kali jawta
Hath barsi dhadha mora
Chala ja bacha charandisa
Akasi mukhi patal ka nasa
Bandh karka naa aoaga to
Mata kali ariki batrish
Dhar pi ka haram koragay

Black bhero with black hair whose hands are set opposite way. You go in the way of man, looking on the sky, but our work should be on the ground. If you become successful then you will be able to drink the milk of mother Kaliari, otherwise if you became a failure then you will be a betrayer to mother kaliyari.

Raipa pir

Bangal sa koun chalu
Raipa pir chalu
Tir kaman hath malata chalu
Dushman hoto laga usko
Mari guru ki ann

Raipa pir

Who has come from the Bengal ?
Raipa Pir has come,
Carrying in his hands bow and arrows ;
Beware Oh enemy,
If you are so, that will hit you
It is my promise
And that too of my Guru.

Procedure

Requirements : A pitcher (unburnt) with a lid, lump of wheat or flower, seven unburnt lamps (made of mud, ghee, wicks for lightint lamp, chicken, bow and arrow (made of stiffy-grass).

Actual Procedure :

The person who desires to execute the above plan has to go inside the deep forest and in that atmosphere of seclusion, he will place the pitcher.

Thereafter, he will keep all the items referred to above one by one simultaneously chanting the hymn. The lump of wheat which was placed inside is required to be pierced with arrow twelve times and also on the body of it, the name of the person concerned ought to be inscribed. Secondly the hen is also required to be pressed into the pitcher and finally close the mouth with the lid. The lighting lamps have already been placed inside the pitcher. The lid of the pitcher is required to be cemented with the lump of wheat in such a manner that there should not be any opening.

The person is now required to leave the pitcher and should not at all take any chance to cast a glance back to the pitcher. If he does so, then he has to invite sufferings under the evil influence of RAIPPA PIR.

The person on whom the magic Raippa Pir is exercised, it is believed, will survive till the chicken inside the pitcher remains alive and he will die with the death of the chicken. The person will die generally suffering from disease like cholera, Bhthysis or blood-dysentery. It is believed by the Bhoksas of Nainital district that in the field of black magic there exists an understanding that the Raippa pir will go ahead while kalua will follow him with a view to assist him.

Kalua

Kala Kalua Kali Rat

Sai Hunkar Andhi Rat

Hat Kara Mamda Bir

Hajir Kha

Chalaja Kalua Unko Pas

Jab Jana Kalua Sacha Bir

Black Kalua
Black night
Howling at mid night
Assisted with Kalua, the black hand
Mahamda Bir and Hazir Kha
Oh Kalua, you go and kill Him (the person aimed at)
Prove your worthiness.

Kalua-II

Bangal sa kaun chalu
Karu Kalua chalu
Dushman ka tai chalu
Mari ann, mari guruki ann
Nann chammariki ann.

Kalua-II

Who has come from the Bengal ?
Black Kalua has come
Moving to kill enemy
It is my promise and that of my Guru
And that too in the name of Namn-chamari.

Two goats and a chopper will be necessary for offering. The person has to go to a far distant place or into the forest alongwith the above requirements. He will sacrifice one goat and chant the hymn in the name of the concerned person. Then the Kalua will rush to the person and kill him. As a token of his execution of the mission, a sign will be visible. (It is said by the Bhoksa Bharara that in the place of magical hymn, a sound of howling will be heard by the observer). Then the other goat is required to offer to him. Otherwise, the Kalua will in turn kill the practitioner. The person concerned on whom the

Kalua magic is applied is supposed to die out of diseases like cholera or blood vomitting.

Manakanjar

Dakshin dashma manakanjar chalu
Hat ma karpa, kala lata chalu
Baat baat mankanjar ish chouk par
Orki chouki torta chalu
Apni chouki lagati chalu
Mari ann, marri guruki ann.

Manakanjar

Manakanjar has come from the south
Saddled with sword and iron rod,
Oh Manakanjar be seated in this Chauki (place)
Move destroying the other chouki
And setting up his own chouki
It is my promise and that too of my Guru.

Requirements : The person is required to collect food begging from virgins, two tortoise, ghee etc.

Actual procedure :

A person who would like to execute the Magic Manakanjar and Nathia kanjar, he should prepare an abode of that which he has taken from the virgin by begging. Then, he has to cut off the head of one of the tortoise and put the same on the *Homam* fire on the abode. The *Homam* fire is prepared by chanting hymn, of Manakanjar and Nathia kanjar in the name of concerned person. The head of the tortoise will have to be burnt till it is reduced to ashes. It is believed that the man will die of asthema. A signal will be visible (a kind of sound resemble the cough of an asthema patient will be heard) on the completion of the work assigned to Manakanjar and Nathia kanjar. Thereafter, another head of the tortoise is required to be offered to the *Homam* fire in the name of the Manakanjar. Otherwise, it is believed by the Bhoksa people that a person who has died by the thrusting paws of a tiger in the jungle or in other places, his soul does not get salvation. This soul roams over the area for peace. If any cattle head or cattle-shed falls on the way of this roaming soul, then this cattle or the cattle of the cattle-shed is affected by this spirit.

An affected cattle of the shed shows the following symptoms :

1. Cattle move their head quickly on both sides from right to left and left to right.

2. The cattle do not take grass as usual.

3. Wind is formed in the belly of the cattle.

4. Sometimes the cattle fall down on the ground.

If the above symptoms are seen by a cattle rearer of the Bhoksas he will identify the situation as an attack of Baghaya spirit. Then the Bhoksa will call a Bharara (sorcerer) of their area. It is also believed that only a Bharara can save the cattle from the evil effects of the Bhagya spirit, only if he is informed at the moment of attack. It is also believed that it will cause immense harm to the practitioner.

Bijlia Khara

Patal sa koun chalu
Takha bir chalu
Mar mar karta chalu
Apni chouki baithata chala
Charpahar din, charpahar rat
Tari chouki tarapahara
Apna pran unka rakhawala

Bijlia Khara

Who has come from the hell ?
Thaka Bir has come
Chanting 'kill him, kill him',
Setting up his own camp
For eight hours in day and eight hours in night,
Guarding the camp himself
Thaka Bir save the pronouncer.

Heart of a frog, hair of a woman are necessary to offer.

A platform is required to be set up in the midst of river in such a way that the man who will sit on it can touch the level surface of water. The man sitting here will place the hair of the woman on the surface of water. It is believed that the hair will convert into snakes on chanting hymns. He is also required to catch one of the snakes twice and on the third occasion, he has to cast the snake in the name of the concerned person. It is firmly believed that the snake will bite the person to which he will succumbed. Thereafter, the snake will return and the offer of the heart of the frog is to be made to him to cause heart failure after the snake will bite the practitioner.

Murga Basikaran

Sita murgi madki dhar
Tujko charao marghatiki ghat
Chalaja narsing baat baat
Ja baithja falna ka ghat
Rotiko manala, sotiko jagala
Jàlsa hil kut-ta aaba
Paban sa dulta aaba

Orko dakhka laga pajaray
Mara dakhka rangsa daray
Falana mantra sribacha
Mari guru sabko acha

Murga basikaran

Sita-the hen is on the verge of death
I shall place you on the Pyre
You the Narashing should move step by step.
And settled yourself to the place of instruction
You don't allow her/him to eat
Awake the sleeping woman/man
She/He will come wading through water
Without caring the attack of cow.

A hole is required to be dug for two hens and some are necessary for prepetuating the act.

During the dark period of the month, the practitioner has to go to a lonely place and has to sacrifice one of the two hens in the name of Narasingh. The blood thus oozing out must be poured into the hole in such a way that it should not sprinkle to his body. The head so cut off will be placed by the side of the *Homa* fire with constant chanting of Hymn. It is believed that the head will fly itself towards the direction of the concerned man. Again, the said head will come back indicating that the job so entrusted to him has been completed.

Now the head of another hen will also be cut off and along with the first one the same should be placed into the hole and thereafter covered with the earth. The Bhoksas believe that it is very strong and effective black magic of making love and if it is acted upon, then no one will escape from its influence.

Tataia

Hari tataia pili tataia
Bish ki raiya
Lagaya tataiya ushko upar
Gorokh ki ann
Falana mantra sribacha
Mari guru sabar sacha

Tataia-I

Green Tataiya, Yello Tataiya
Carrying poison
Go and sitting him
It is in the name of Garakhnath
This hymn is true
Being my Guru the best.

Tataia-II

Hari tataiya pili tataiya
Bishki raiya
Utarja bish tataiya
Gorokh ki ann.
Atna bish na utaraba to
Tara Dobi ki do babay
Dobaga marangi
Mari guru sabar sacha

Tataiya-II

Green Tataiya, Yellow Tataiya
Carrying poison
On Tataiya retreat from him

It is in the name of Garakhnath
This hyme is true, being my Guru the best.

Tumri-I

Arghat ki tumri
Marghat ki baayn
Barja tumri
Khichla pran.

Tumri-I

Tumri of Arghat
Flue of burialghat
Oh Tumri you go
And put him on the verge of death.

Tumri-II

Arghat ki tumri
Marghat ki Baayan
Nikalja tumri
Bachala pran

Tumri II

Tumri of Arghat
Flute of Burial ghat
Oh Tumri you retreat
Save him from death.

Manakanjar

Baro ghat bangalia
Jaha kaha manakanjar
Tinshow sat cosh dhora damna
Kiya latahua chala

Paban bidya

Hatsa barsha lata chala
Mar mar karta chala
Apni chouki baithath chala
Orki chouki torta chala
Falana mantra sribacha
Mari guru sabar achaha

Manakanjar

Oh Manakanjar Bangalia of Baru ghat
Where are you going
Stretching over 360 miles area
And what are you carrying?
Is it art of Air
Go on carrying spear
Go on devastating
Go on setting up own camp.

Narsing :

Kamrud desh ka kamanta devi
Ushma baisa ashman jogi
Ashman jogi na bai bari
Ful bina nan-chammari
Akk ful hasha akh ful baisa
Hasha ful ma narsing baisa
Ja sukhiba fulki bass
Sa abagi mari pas
Falna mantra sa sachcha
Mari guru ki bat sachcha.

Kamantadevi of Kamrupdesh

There too lived Ashman Jogi

There he sets up an Ashram

Where you can not witness Mannchamari without flowers.

The flower smiles and other withers

Narasingh sits on the smiling flower

And she who smells that flowers

Has to rush to me

This hyme is best of all

And this is the prediction of my guru

It is nothing but true.

Kali-I

Kali kali mahakali

Indraki bati bramaki sali

Chaba pan bajaba tali

Rang rong kara rakhowali

Kali-I

Kali Kali Mahakali

Daughter of Indra and sister-in-law of Brahma

Chewing betle leaves, beating the plate

Preserving the world

Utang Rang, Rung (two hymic words).

Kali-II

Kali Kalkata bali kali

Atong motanaka pakhawali bali kali

Bhut prat mar ka samao

Bandana labagi

Calcutta Kali bali kali-
Who sway over the world
Driving away the Ghost-spirits-demons, etc.
Freed him from the influence of evil.

Bhero

Agad bhero jagai bhero
Char chandali chandal bhero
Ulta ganga olta nir
Ulta mara chousat-
Jalbani basan bir
Mari bandana bandhoko
Sri Ramchandra nann mat bir ki dohay
Sat guru ki dohaiy

Bhero

Agad Bhero and Gagat Bhero
Four Chandali with chandal Behro
Water of Ganga flows reversely
64 Brahman Birs are also shaped reversely
If you don't obey me
At least you comply to Ramchandra, the God
And also to my God blessed Guru

Bhero-I

Kali bhero kari jata
Mach machi ka bhojon kha
Ishki dishak ban do
Mari an, mari guruki ann.
Nanchamari ki ann.

Bhero-I

Black Bhero with curling hair
With ear ring that looks beautiful
He eats fish
I say you capture the mind of the unknown woman
This is in the name of my guru
and that too in the name of Nanchamari.

Bhero-II

Kali bhero kumri jata
Mach machi ka bhojan kha
Ishki dishak ban do
Mari ann, mari guruki ann
Nanchamari ki ann.

Bhero-II

Black Bhero with matted hair
Consumes males and fish
Sterile her mind
This is in the name of myself
and that too my guru and Nanchamari

Saiyad

Nila gora pila palash
Upar uta mogol pathan
Gag gag saiyad barni
Bhut ki patko marko
Mashan ko sab ko mar ko
Orki chouki torti ja
Apni chouki banat ja
Twenty two khooja ka dohai

Saiyad

Blue Bhero with yellow eyes
Magal and Pathan are powerful
Awake Saiyad
Killing the Ghost and Spirits
Specially the ghosts of burning place
Demolishing the other camp
Establishing your own
Otherwise you are answerable to 22 Khoaja.

X

Jungle spirits

Bhoksa inhabited villages are generally found on the foot-hills of the Himalayas. The villages are found near a forest. The Bhoksas are reputed for their skill in leading life in the forest area. In other words, the tradition of the Bhoksa community are tuned with the sylvan settings. Their day-to-day contact with forest has developed into their mind a strong belief that some spirits and ghosts are in the forest who can do harm as well as good to them. Among the forest spirits and ghosts some of them are malevolent in nature. They only do harm to the people in different ways and others are benevolent in nature doing good to them. These benevolent spirits work for the welfare of the community. Majhi is one of the malevolent spirits as believed by the Bhoksa people of Nainital District. If anybody comes under the influence of this spirits, then it is assumed that this person would die within a few days. Even if he stays in house, considering the Majhi could not affected him he will die. The Majhi tries to get him out of the house by calling in a voice of his dearest friend at the dead part of the night. It is believed by them if the person comes out hearing the voice of his friend, then he will be in the trap of the Majhi and if he does not go outside the room then and then only he is saved. It is also further believed that the Majhi has no power to do harm to anybody who is in a room. It is the household gods and goddesses who can guard the inmates of the house from the evil eye of the Majhi. But the Majhi tries to do harm to that person till he is not free from the influence and neutralised by the Bharara, the sorcerer of the area. All the community members are afraid of the bad influence of the Majhi.

Another malevolent spirit is Okhaya. Okhya is found in the forest as believed by the Bhoksa of Nainital district. This spirit is not as harmful as the Majhi is. This spirit rules over the jungle area. This spirit could effect a person who is not in the forest and he does not attack a group of persons. It is believed by the community members that anybody who can, under the influence of Okhaya, lose his way out in the midst of forest. Even a reputed person who work as a guide of the forest since long past can also lose his way under the influence of the Okhaya. The man has to spend day or days together in the forest till a group rescues him from the jungle. Okhaya does not kill anybody. But he makes a fun with a person by making him suffer from being without food, drinks and also by putting him in uncertainty and making him anxious for his life. If the friends or villagers do not rescue him, then he may die of starvation. For these reasons, the Bhoksas go in a gang to collect wood in the forest. All the persons of the gang are instructed by elder members to move in the forest jointly for collecting dry wood, honey, etc. Similarly, the Bhoksa of Dehra Dun district believe in Saiyad. It is said by the Bhoksas of Dehra Dun district that if Saiyad is not pleased with a person, then it is very difficult for that person to return from the forest. He either is attacked by the wild animals or he may meet with sudden accident. So, it is very dangerous for the man, who has regular connection with the forest, to incur displeasure of Saiyad. Therefore the Bhoksa of Dehra Dun district worship Saiyad and tries to get his favour because he rules over the forest. Baiwala is a reputed benevolent jungle spirit believed by the Bhoksa community of Nainital district. It is believed that she helps her worshipper to find out lost cattle from the jungle. When the cattle go astray, the Bhoksa make promise to the spirit Baiawala that they will offer her pork, if she can find out their lost cattle. Apart from that, he is quite popular for her good deeds. People also frequently propitiate the spirit and never forget to keep their promise to this spirits.

During the field investigation, the fieldworker got a scope to witness the villagers worshipping this spirit. Sobbi sing of Pipalsanna village of Ramnagar Block of Nainital district lost a cow while he lets his own cows out for grazing in the forest. After searching for this lost cow for days together when he failed to get any trace of his cow, he promised to the spirit Baiawala to offer a pig if she finds his cow in safe and sound. Luckily, he got back his cow from the jungle after three days. According to them, this is the proof of her effectiveness. It is also believed by them that failure to fulfill one's promise after achieving success may bring a heavy loss to the offender. Therefore, they are promt in fulfilling their promise to offer a pig in the name of Baiawala even on the very day of achieving success.

In Dehra Dun district, Saiyad is treated as a forest ghost. In every forest there are some alters of Saiyad, which are made of mud with an elevation of

1'x 2' with a breadth of one foot. Some of the alters are made of bricks with plaster of cement. They say that this is the place of Saiyad. If anybody enters into the forest for any work, then he should beg of Saiyad for his safety there. It is believed by them that if Saiyad is pleased with a person, then he is free from danger in the forest, such as, attack of wild animal, failing from the tree, snake bite etc. If Saiyad is displeased, then it becomes troublesome for him to come out from the jungle safely. Bhoksas of Dehra Dun district are the regular visitors of the forest. They collect forest products like Bind-grass (a kind of grass which is available in the deep forest), leaves (which they use for preparing plate), dry wood, and wood for the construction of the new houses or to repair the old ones. They offer to Saiyad, 'Mithachawal' once in a year. There is no group function to worship Saiyad. One may worship Saiyad at any time when one is capable of doing it. Generally, offering to Saiyad is done in the month of Baisak. Bhoksas have their regular contact with this portion of the forest, particularly in the second half of the day. In the first half, adult males are engaged in the agricultural fields, whereas adult females are busy with the household activities. So, only in the second half, they get time to go into the forest with their domestic animals for grazing. But in agricultural seasons, when all the adult males or females are fully engaged, then children generally go into this part of the forest with their cattle for grazing. Ordinarily the young school-going children have to perform this job of herding their domestic animals for helping their families. This part of the forest is not rich in edible roots or fruits or firewood, because due to regular grazing of cattle these do not get a chance to grow. Besides, the herdsman, if they find any fruit or root, they collect it. In the middle part of the forest, which is next to the upper part of the forest, the men or women usually go for collecting dry wood for fuel or for collecting wooden poles for reconstruction of old houses or to construct new ones. Generally, the Bhoksa women do the job of collecting fuel wood and at the same time they also eollect roots, tubers, fruits, barks, etc. which they find in this part of the forest. Sometimes one or two male persons go into this part accompanying their women as guides or as escorts. For the collection of wooden poles, one or more goups of men go together in a gang into the forest and select the required wooden poles, they cut them down and return home with the wooden poles. The lower part of the forest is treated as the interior part as well as the dangerous part of all their accessible portion of the forest. In the period from August to September, they go into this part in a group for collecting the *Bindgrass, Munch,* and *Chalta.* Generally, every year they visit this part of the forest once or twice and sometimes more, depending on their requirment. Neither the women nor the young children or a person alone is allowed to visit this part of the forest. It is because this part of the forest is full of wild animals and they may attack any time.

Due to their living in the proximity of the forest, the tradition of the Bhoksa community is tuned to the environment of the forest. Their day-to-day contact with the forest has forced them to develop a strong belief that some spirits are in the forest which can do harm and can also do good to them. Among the forest spirits some are malevolent by nature. They harm the people according to nature. They work in favour of the people in case they are pleased over them.

According to them the accessible parts of the forest are ruled by the three benevolent spirits, they are *Bhagaya, Okhaya* and *Majhi* and one benevolent spirit, *i.e.*, Sarawala. Spirit Bhagaya is well known for its benevolent nature. Though it won't directly affect man, yet its affect comes on the society of the Bhoksa people in a harmful way. It may do harm to the cattle also. It is believed that a person, who is killed by a tiger, his soul transforms into a Ghagaya spirit. At the time of roaming of the soul of this spirit, if any cattle or a number of cattle fall on its way, then the cattle can get affected by its malevolent nature. A cattle affected by the harmful nature of this spirit falls on the ground and dies. But, it is also believed by the Bhoksa people that only the Bharara, a local sorcerer, can save the cattle from the effects of Bhagaya, if he is informed in time.

The spirit, Majhi, is a malevolent spirit. This spirit is malevolent to the mankind. It is believed that the Majhi is the soul of men or women who died of accidents in the forest or outside the forest. If anybody falls under the influence of this malevolent spirit, then it is assumed that the person will die within a few days, even if he stays in his house in the hope that Majhi can not affect him. Majhi pretends to call him in a voice of his dearest friend at the dead of night and calls him out. Hearing the voice of a friend if he does not go outside the house, then only he may save himself because Majhi has no power to do harm to anybody inside a room. The Bhoksas are sacred of the bad influence of Majhi.

XI

Spirit *OKHAYA* is malevolent to the mankind, but not so harmful as Majhi. It is believed by the Bhoksa people that if a man dies in the forest without getting food and water, then the soul of this dead person transforms into a Okhaya spirit. This spirit rules over the jungle only, outside the jungle it has no power at all; it can not affect a gang of persons. If anybody falls under the influence of Okhaya spirit, then he loses his way leading out from the forest, however he may be a man of reputation for his skill in the jungle. The man has to spend a day or days together in the forest till his friends come to rescue him from the forest. Spirit Okhaya does not kill anybody directly, he only makes fun with a person by making him suffer for food, drinking water and by keeping him in anguish and uncertainty of life.

The spirit Baiwala is a spirit reputed for its good deeds. This spirit helps her worshippers in finding out a cattle from the jungle which might have lost while grazing in the forest. It is believed by the Bhoksa that this spirit is the soul of a virtous woman or Padhania (wife of the village head) of the village. She helps her villagers by dint of her heavenly affections towards her villagers. When a cow or buffalo goes astray, then the Bhoksa make a promise to this spirit for her worship if the lost animal is found. She is quite popular for her good deeds as she delivers the goods and is frequently propitiated by them.

XII

Although the Bhoksa believe that all these four spirits rule the accessible parts of the forest, yet the natures and activities of these spirits reveal that each of these spirits has certain link up with a particular part of the forest. The attack of Bhagaya spirit is reported to be prevalent in the upper part, i.e., the part near to a locality of the forest. Thus, the attacks of the spirits, the Okhaya and the Majhi, are reported to be more frequent in the middle and the lower parts of the forest, respectively. So, it is in the fitness of things that the belief concerning the forest spirits in relation to the natural environment has some direct or indirect link with the different parts of the forest which is to be taken under consideration from the empirical knowledge.

The spirit Bhagaya harms the cattle. The cattle are reared in the upper part of the forest. So the scope of attack on a cattle by the Bhagaya spirit is only possible in the upper part of the forest. Owing to the proximity of the village and due to their frequent contacts with the upper part of the forest the Bhoksa feel most secured in this part of the forest though, according to them, influence of the spirits like the Okhaya and the Majhi is there. Due to grazing of their cattle they keep an eye on their cattle, so that they are not lost. However, the spirit Biawala is there to protect the cattle from the apprehended loss. Actually, the upper part of the forest is not so thick and finding a lost cattle head in this part is not impossible. However, their belief of spirits have made an adjustment with the natural setting of the forest. The middle part of the forest is meant for collection of dry wood or wooden beams. The collection may be done in a group, but this may lead to a dispute among the members of the group over the choice for better dry wood or for the good quality beams. At the same time, it is not expected that sufficient dry wood for the group may be available at one place. They have to move here and there in search of the required forest products. So, the spirit Okhaya may get scope of attack to a person in this part of the forest when a person moves alone into deep forest for collection of the required forest products and it is not improbable for a person to get lost in the forest or being attacked by wild animals such as bear, tiger etc. So, the belief of Okhaya spirit forces them to work in a group and to prepare them mentally to cope with the unexpected danger of the forest. The Okhsas are tremendously scared of evil tendencies of Majhi spirit. The Majhi can attack a person even if he is in a group. The Bhoksa go into the lower part of the forest only in the months of August and September. This is the period when sufficiently the required materials are available within a limited area. As described earlier, the lower part of the forest is infested with wild animals such as tiger, elephant, and other animals and also by the Majhi spirit. So, the lower part of the forest may be considered as dangerous spot in the light of the belief of spirit and also due to the preponderance of wild animals.

From the above discussion it may be said that the belief of a particular spirit is linked with particular part of the forest. As they go into the depth of the forest, the belief concerning spirits which ruled this part is that they are more dangerous than those who rule the adjacent parts of the forest where wild animals are not in abundance. Now, it is not unlikely to conjecture that the belief of spirit and natural environment of the forest are interdependent to each other. Their belief of the spirit that in anticipation gives their community members a scope to adjust themselves with probable risks or dangers of the accessible parts of the forest environment and help them to collect the forest products safely.

Spirits and ghosts have also taken their position in the cattle-shed of the Bhoksa community. Both the malevolent and benevolent spirits and ghost are found to influence the cattle of the Bhoksas of Nainital district. Among these spirits and ghosts, Bagaya is a spirit of malevolent nature and is very harmful to cattle.

XII

There is another ghost or spirit found prevalent among the Bhoksa of Nainital district, which is called *Barsi*. This ghost or spirit does not harm the villagers or mankind. According to the Bhoksa, when a pregnant woman dies, they cut the belly of the pregnant woman and cremate the mother and child separately. The soul of that woman with its affection towards the child move searching for her child at dead part of the night. The Bhoksa of Nainital district say that sometimes at deep night, some light may be seen in the fields where the dead body is cremated. They belief that this is Barsi who searcher her child for giving milk. If any pregnant woman gets murdered, then her soul turns into a dangerous spirit, called *chourel*. This soul is very harmful towards mankind. If anybody falls under the grip of *chourel* then it is only the *Bharara* who can save him or her from the hand of Chourel by his mysterious power.

Chapter - Eight

TRADITIONAL VILLAGE COUNCILS AND JUDICIARY SYSTEM

I

The Bhoksa villages of Nainital district are organised under their three traditional institutions, viz., *Podhan* (authority of 'gott' or clan members), *Ponch* headed by Khum-Podhan (village level controlling institution) and *Takat* (inter-village controlling institution headed by Takat). Whereas in Dehradun district, only two institutions are found, *i.e.*, Podhan (the authority of 'gott' or clan members) and the *Panch* (the village level council headed by Prodhan) to control and maintain law and order in the society.

Podhan is the head of a sub-group or clan and has usually comes from the eldest members of the sub-groups. He is supposed to be a founder-members of the village. The post of Podhan has the authority as well as the prestige of his office to maintain cohesion, solidarity and discipline of the sub-group members in the village. If any dispute arises among the sub-group members, or with members of other sub-groups, then it is the Podhan of the concerned sub-groups who is supposed to know the fact first. If this case is within the group, the Podhan with other senior members of the sub-groups, takes initiative to solve the matters through mutual understanding (adjustment of the involved parties). If it is a case of inter-clan dispute, then the members of each clan make their respective Podhan aware of the facts, who is one of the selected members of the *Panch.* His consent is important to satisfy a case and to win the case at *panch.* In fact, podhan is the friend, philosopher and guide of the sub-group members among the Bhoksa. He is expected to head on social occasion, such as marriage, get-together, and other social occasion of the clan members.

The Khum-Podhan is the traditional village head. The office of the Khum-Podhan was actually created by the British Government Administration to develop the area and for better administration of the area. The Khum Podhan was appointed by the Khum-authorities which was established by the British administration to develop the tarai region. The Khum Podhan was accountable to Khum authorities. He was responsible for the distribution of land to the villagers and collect revenue from the villagers. In the case of larger settlement, there used to be a number of Podhan operative in the area, but one of them who was the most powerful or vocal and capable person used to speak for all Podhan of the particular region. The office of the Khum Podhan is a respected one. He holds a good position in the village. As he looks after the village and villagers, the alter of the village and that of 'Vimsen' are situated in front of the Podhan's house.

As in Nainital district, the conception of village head as Podhan is not prevalent among the Bhoksas of Dehra dun district. Actually their settlement was establish by the influence of zamindar. A zamindar selects a man to be a group leader or Podhan of the village who had the capacity to control the village. He was supposed to work in favour of the zamindar and collect due share of the crops. If any dispute arised within the village, the Podhan of the village had the authority to solve its consulting other villagers of the village. He used to give his views to solve a case. His opinion is the final verdict of the case. If the Podhan favoured wrongly a group, nobody dared object his opinion. They had no courage and unity to inform of the matter to the court of the zamindar.

II

Panch is the village level organization that exercises control over the affairs of the village. Through the panch, the village-head or *Khum* head or *podhan* controls and maintains discipline in the village. Podhans of each sub-group is a members of the *panch.* The *Khum-podhan* is the traditional village head. The office of the khum-podhan was actually created by the British Government to develop the area and for the better administration of the area. The khum-podhan was appointed by the *Khum* authorities which was establish by the British Government (administration) to develop the tarai region. The Podhan was accountable to khum authorities. He was responsible for the collection and distribution of the land to villagers and collect revenue from the villagers.

Panch generally dealt with social problems. The eldest of members of each clan or lineage become the exofficio members of the panch. In case of a inter-clan conflict, the representatives of both the clans try to highlight the case in favur of their clan through the panch. First, podhans hear the allegation of the representative parties, after hearing the facts and circumstances of conflict, the podhan awards his verdict about the case in consultation with other members of the panch. Generally, the panch deals with a case sympathitically, considering the effects of the case in social affairs. If the case is of a conflict between two parties, the panch calls the representative families involved in the case and mutual understanding is brought about. If the case concern social affairs and affects the custom of the society, then the case is treated strongly and the parties involved are punished. The guilty person/s are simultaneously subjected to fine as well as social boycott. Generally, the panch deals with the cases of divorce, remarriage elopment of a girl, affairs of love, and pre-marital or extra-marital sex relations.

III

Takat panchayat is a inter-village and intra-village institution through which the Bhoksa of Nainital district seek justice. Takat panchayat is headed by the Takat and the khum-podhan of each village. Takat panchyat deals with a case of inter village dispute. It becomes operative only in the case of a conflict between the khum-podhan and any villager of the same khum-podhan's village. Takat panchayat is the supreme authority of the area. Verdict of this panchayat is final and it is supposed to be obeyed by all members of the community. Takat panchayat has the authority to excommunicate any one from the village or from the community by way of punishment. In Nainital district, three Takat panchayats are found functioning, viz., (1) the eastern Takat which is headed by Chandan Singh, whose headquarters is at Gatherpur, Chandan Singh lives in the village of Kopa-Kripali of Gathepur block; (2) Central Takat, the head-quarters of Central Takat is at Chandanpur. The Central Takat covers a vast area between Kosi and Ghagara river. Chandan Singh of the Baria-Dawalat Halt is the headquarters of the Central Takat. This Takat consists of 52 villages and (3) the Northern Takat which is headed by Bhoora Singh of Birpur Tara with its headquarters' at village Birpur Tara of Ramnagar Block. This Takat consists of 20 villages. Among the Takats, the Central Takat is the largest and the Northern Takat is the smallest one.

The office of the traditional Takat has four office bearers. The head of the Takat panchayat is termed as Takat who is assisted by Munsif as adviser. *Daroga* is the chief executive officer. *Nai* is the massenger. At present, the office of the Nai has been abolished, but the *Sepai* is now doing the job of Nai. The inter-village Takat is headed by the chief who is designated as Takat. He is assisted by the *munsif*, who gives advice to the Takat and assists him to disposes of the cases. *Daroga* is the chief executive officer of the Takat. He summons the parties to a meeting and ensures compliance of decision of Takat. Sepai is the messanger to convey message to the contending parties. Sepai also executes the punishments inflicted by the Takat.

Village Pipal-sanna of Ramnagar Block of Nainital district comes under the preview of the northern Takat. Bhoora singh of Birpur Tara village holds the post of Takat of northern Takat. Sarup Singh of Thari village holds the post of Munsif. Guman Singh of Baria village holds the post of Daroga and Lalsing of Lalitpur village holds the post of Sepai of Northern Panchayat. The Khum-Podhan of the villages are the members of the Takat Panchayat by virtue of their position. The Central Takat covers the vast area of Bazpur Block of Nainital district. The head of the Takat Panchayat is Chandan Singh. He lives in village Chandanpur.

When the podhan fails to settle a case satisfactorily in panch, then he refers the matter to Takat. The concerned parties, then can approach the Takat.

When any of the contending parties is dissatisfied with the decision of the village head or panch, then that party is free to take the issue to Takat. In that case, it is obligatory for the said party to seek permission of the Khum-podhan. It is to be mentioned here that the accused party, by the judgement of the Takat, will have to pay the expenses of the Takat. In the past, Takat panchayat generally dealt with the following.

1. Land and crops disputes.
2. Disputes relating to Canal water and irrigation water.
3. Marriage dispute.
4. Theft and cattle lifting.
5. Sex offences.
6. Inheritance of property.
7. Divorce.
8. Remarriage.

In the past, traditional Takat panchyat also dealt with cases considering its effects on society. Theft and sexual offences are regarded as serious crime because theft directly damages property and sexual offence discriminates the status of men and women. In case of therft, a fine is imposed on the guilty party and sometimes physical humulation is also inflicted. Sexual offence is treated strictly; at first they try to find out the guilty person, then they impose social boycott on both the parties. In case of involvement of an unmarried girl, compensation is to be paid by the involved male person for the marriage of the girl. Sometimes the involved male is made to carry torn shoes in his mouth. At times, the male person is humilated by excommunication. Takat can punish the guilty women also. At present

Takat is acting in its natural form, but it deals only with the social affairs. Now they are not dealing with any case arising out of theft, land dispute and conflicts over the distribution irrigation water etc. The main duty of the present Takat is to keep up harmony between the groups. Now the Takats are dealing with the cases of social offences, such as, extra-marital sex relation, marriage disputes, divorce, remarriage and elopment of girl etc.

Traditional Bhoksa Council never deals with any case of murder. In such an event, the village head or khum-podhan immediately brings the matter to the notice of the khum-superintendent of the area who is the competent legal authority to handle such cases. The Bhoksas of Dehradun district do not have such an organised Panchayat. Their only Panchayat is the Panch. Sometimes, influence of the leader of a clan crosses the boundary of the village. Importance of the eldest person of the clan members is significant. When any conflict arises among the groups, it is solved by the clan members or by the village Panch. If they fail, then they refer the case to the Zamindar's court. As in Nainital, Dehradun Bhoksa Council never deals with a case of murder. In the case of any murder or theft, they refer it to the court of the zamindar.

IV

The Statutory Council came into being in the Bhoksa society after the promulgation of the U.P. Panchayat Raj Act, in 1948. A village or a group of villages, when satisfy the required population criteria mentioned for the purpose of constitution, the Gaon Panchayat is formed. Gaon Panchayat Sabha consists of all the individuals, irrespective of sex or age, of 18 years and above. One or more Gaon panchayat constitute a Naya- panchayat. The traditional panchayat (such as panch) in Dehradun district and (Panch and Takat in Nainital district) handle both the judicial and the administrative functions which are run by separate bodies. The judicial is performed by the Naya-panchayat and the executive function is performed by the Gaon Panchayat. Members of these panchayats are elected through adult franchise. The Bhoksa village (pipal sanna) of Ramnagar Block of Nainital district come under the Gaon Sabha constituency consisting of five villages, *i.e.*, pipal-sanna, Rajpur, Lalitpur Kamdebpur, Sakhanpur, Prem Sing, a Bhoksa of Pipal sanna village, is the elected podhan of this constituency. He has been holding the post of podhan since panchayat election came into being. The post of this constituency of Gaon-sabha is treated as reserved for scheduled tribe. This constituency of Gaon sabha has come under the Naya-panchayat constituency of Chilkia of Ramnagar Block, which is headed by the Sarpanch. Naya panchayat constituency of Chilkia consists of ten Gaon sabha and every Gaon sabha has two members in the Naya panchayat as representatives of the selected Gaon sabha. The elected members of the Pipal-sanna village are the representatives of the Bhoksa people in Naya panchayat. The Khum-bari village of Bazpur Blocks of Nainital district comes under the Khum-bari Gaon-sabha constituency. In this Gaon-sabha constituency Kuwrar Singh, a Bhoksa of Khum-bari, is the elected podhan. He has been holding the post of Gaon-sabha since panchayat election came into being. All villages of Gaon sabha are dominated by the Bhoksa people. This constituency of the Gaon sabha comes under the Naya-panchayat constituency of Ban-khera of Bazpur Block which is headed by the Sarpanch and assisted by Assistant Sarpanch. Every Gaon sabha has two members as a representative in Naya-panchayat. Elected members of the Khumbari Gaon sabha and also other Bhoksa dominated Gaon sabha are the representatives of the Bhoksa people in Naya-panchayat. In the Tiparpur Gaon sabha, Cimmanlal - a Bhoksa, is the elected podhan of the village. In the past, this post of podhan was hold by a Gujar. The Naya panchayat constituency, to which the studied village belongs is the Sahaspur constituency. The Naya panchayat constituency is headed by the Sarpanch and also Assisted by Assistant Sarpanch. Every Gaon sabha has two members to represent Gaon sabha in Naya panchayat.

Naya panchayat of both the districts is assisted by the panchayat secretary, who is a government body of the B.D.O. office. His duty is to help the village panchayat in carrying out their duties in conformity with regulation. Influence of statutory panchayat is remarkable to the village of Dehradun district. Bhoksas of Dehradun believe that the statutory (panchayat) council can work more fruitfully than the traditional panch. Whereas, the Bhoksa of Nainital district rely more on the judgement of the traditional panchayat, such as, Panch and Takat, their views toward the present statutory panchayat is not favoured by them. This panchayat favours the other group of people whose members hold a venerable position in this panchayat.

The Gaon Sabha has administrative duties and power to deal with the public affairs which are usually taken up by the traditional panch, including management of public organisations and public property, celebration of festivals and the execution of development measures introduced by the Government with regard to the communities in the village. The Naya panchayat is purely a judicial body with power to maintain law and order. Naya panchayat has the authority to levy fines upto a sum of rupees five hundred. When a dispute arises among the members of the village, the involved parties usually inform the podhan of the Gaon Sabha. After getting information of conflict, the podhan circulates a notice informing all the Gaon sabha members, mentioning the date of sitting of the panchayat. The panchayat podhan with other members of the Gaon sabha tries to solve the problem amicably. If the podhan fails to resolve the case, then he refers the matter to Naya panchayat. If the Naya panchayat fails to solve the problem, then the panchayat refers it to court. The statutory panchayat has no authority to dispose of any murder case or some such incidents. The Gaon sabha then immediately brings the case to the notice of the police who is the competent authority to handle such matters.

The elites constitute the reservior, out of which the leadership may be drawn and they have always the potential for becoming leaders. As mentioned before, the endogamous Bhoksa society is segmented into a number of sub-groups. Gotra or clan plays a significant role in their social structure. There is also a recognized link among the groups through Khera-the place of their original habitation. So, their respective sub-groups heads or clan heads or Khera heads are the traditional elites whose voice has some weight among the Bhoksa community. The sub-group heads and also village heads (Khum-podhan) are holding respectable positions in their society. As their society do not maintain any hierchial stratification, the social work or service for the community is the main source of gaining popularity to become an elite of the society. The Khum-podhan or the village and the Takat podhan of the community are still holding respectable position of their society and are also obeyed by the villagers and the community members. In the case of Khum-podhan (village head), some religious as well as sentimental or psychological assignment is present which is related to the traditional Khum-podhan or a village head. In the past, he was the friend, philosopher and guide among them. He distributes lands among them and make necessary arrangement for the welfare of the villagers at the time of their difficulties. At present, only village head (Khum-podhan) has the right to worship the Bhumsen (the village god) and also in Khera *pujan*. Khera is the community goddess for the welfare of the villagers and community members.

Takat head, the head of inter-village panchayat still holds a respected position. The view of Takat is taken for granted by the community. They believe that through the Takat Panchayat their community can maintain distinction and solidarity of the community members. If the solidarity of the community is broken, then their society will break in the near future. So, they respect Takat head and his views regarding political matters also. At present, some educated young men are trying to raise their voice in the social and political affairs. But their voices are accepted only if the traditional leaders accept their views. Otherwise, they have to face their traditional Council and sometimes they are punished by the traditional Panchayat for their doing so.

The establishment of U. P. Land Tenancy Act and the abolition of Zamindary system, demarcated to a great extent the power and authority of the village heads. The traditional elite groups or their family members or lineage members are now acting as present elite groups. Traditional Panch heads are at present the elected heads of both statutory panchayat and the Gaon panchayat. In fact, the traditional panch members are the members of the Statutory Panchayat or are elected with the consent of the traditional village head. So, statutory Gaon panchayats are nothing but a new form of old panchayat. The only difference is that the old panch was operative within one village, but the Gaon Sabha operates over one or more villages. It is found that generally in the Naya panchayat, the posts of Sarpanch and Assistant Sarpanch are held by the people other than Bhoksa, such as, Panjabi or any other community. Some of the Bhoksa village heads are also the members of any community other than Bhoksa. But in such cases, support of the traditional Bhoksa leader is needed.

At present, some of the young Bhoksas are would-be political elites. They have acquired good reputation among the Bhoksa and also other communities for their good conduct. These young people have a good traditional background as well as sound economic position. They are educated and have power of speaking with high government officials. They always visit the Bhoksa area and enquire into their difficulties and try to solve their problems. Some traditional leaders are however not pleased with them. But, these people are more or less attached with the "Servants of India Society". This Society works in the area of Bazpur and Ramnagar for the development of the tribals. So, the views of the Secretary of the Servants of India Society are always accepted by the traditional leaders.The young people who are thus attached with the organisation are more or less accepted by the Bhoksa community members in political affairs.

The traditional Bhoksa leaders are, at present, of the opinion that it is meet and proper to elect educated youngmen as the functionaries of their community who have good economic condition, honesty, popularity as a good social worker and have the organizing ability and also are capable of dealing with government officials for their problems.

The Bhoksas at large are depending more on the leadership of young people now than the aged traditional leaders, who are submissive to the external pressures created by other communities. They can not adequately face problems developing and turn against the changes that have taken place recently. In accepting an young man as a leader, they lookout for some good qualities in him. In case of an young man who is from the family of a Podhan, (traditional village head) the acceptance comes easily. But when a young man who has no such back-ground needs to have a good number of other qualities to become a leader.

In Dehradun district the Bhoksas have adopted the Statutory Panchayat as the only recognised political platform. But still they are not out of the clutches of the traditional political system. Podhan is still being venerated by the villagers. The Podhan and his lineage plays an important role in running the present political system. In Tiparpur village, the past Gaon Sabha Podhan was a Gujar of the same village. Although the Gujars form a small population of the village, yet they established their per-dominance over the Bhoksa population in elections. In the previous election, Chamanlal, a Bhoksa, was able to have the group support and won the election. Other communities, such as, Baniyas being traders by caste, and Harijans belonging to lower stratum of the social hierarchy, sometimes support the Gujar leaders to win. In the Tiparpur village, it is found that there is always existence of political tension between the Bhoksa and Gujars. They also try to justify their activities for the development of the community as well as of the village.

VI

Traditional Takat panchayat is still active to play its role in social matters, such as, marriage, divorce, elopment etc. and inter-village and intra-village conflicts are still resolved in the Takat panchayat. At present Takat Panchayat and the present statutory panchayat are working side by side in close cooperation. In case of intra-community disputes Takat panchayat resolves the disputes effectively. When the case is a inter-community one then the case is solved in Gaon Sabha level. Actually, the village head or lineage members of the past head are now the elected members of the Statutory Panchayat. Traditional leaders of the Bhoksa such as, the Podhan, Takat, Munsif, Darga, Sipai-all are eager to get elected as members of the Statutory Panchayat, because the Statutory Panchayat members hold more respected position than that of traditional panchayat. The present Statutory Panchayat members have the scope to come closes to the government official, such as, B.D.O., A.D.O., Panchayat secretary etc. and other prominent leaders of the area. The Bhoksas of Nainital district are organised under a institution named "Bhoksa Parisad". The headquarters of the Bhoksa Parisad is situated in village Baria-Daulat. The Parisad was established in the year 1965-66. This institution was created with a view to develop the Bhoksas educationally, economically and politically. To achieve the goal, the Parisad has set up a library, a debating centre and a recreation centre for the community. In order to train the Bhoksas in agriculture and craftmanship, instructors have been engaged. To impart knowledge in agricultural techniques, an agricultural expert has been appointed. Similarly, to train them in small scale and cottage industries there is another expert. The Parishad also keeps and account of census done on the Bhoksas of the villages of the surrounding areas.

The executive body of the organisation consists of 11 members, among whom Narayan Datta Tiwari, is the organiser of the Bhoksa Parisad. The other main executive Bhoksa members are :

1. Ram Sing - Cashier.
2. Bhola Dharambir - Secretary of the organisation.

Any Bhoksa may become a member of the Bhoksa Parisad after paying Rs. 10/- to the organisation as admission fee. This Parisad is keenly interested in the economic and social well-being of the Bhoksa. To get their lands back, which they have lost due to indebtedness, either to Government or to any person, the Parisad is trying its level best and for this purpose the Parisad is regularly communicating with the Chief Minister of the U.P. mentionning their problems about lands and other difficulties, which they face in day-to-day life. Although this Parisad wants to fight for the development of the community, yet this Parisad is gradually losing its membership strength and support of the Bhoksa community due to some conflict in the executive body of the Bhoksa Parisad. An influencial Bhoksa leader, Udai Singh, of Mazra-Pachue village is now trying to re-establish the Bhoksa Parisad again. He visits villages of Ramnagar, Bazpur, Gadharpur Blocks and discusses with the traditional leaders about the "Bhoksa Parisad" and its aims and objectives. He tries to increase the number of membership of the Bhoksa Parisad. He says, if the Bhoksas can not organize themselves at this moment, then they will not be able to hold the lands. The outsiders who come in Tarai, will rule their area in the near future.

VII

In the Bhoksa society, the social structure shows some kind of interdependence among the lineage members and also the 'gotra' or clan members. The endogamous Bhoksas community is segmented into a number of sub-groups and their respective sub-groups lineage members have some link with the lineage head and also with the gotra head. They are holding respectable positions and their suggession are sometimes given weitage by sub-groups or members. The podhan of the village or the Takat podhan of the community have their respective suggestions for the welfare of the community. In case of the village-head, some religious as well as sentimental or psychological assignment is related with the prestige of the village-head and also with the village. In such informal cases the present educated young persons have no say in the matter. Sometimes they have to obey the guidance and instructions of the village head without any hesitation for fear of difficulty in some social obligations, otherwise he would be punished by the panchayat through ex-communication.

Promulgation of U.P. Land Tenancy Act and the abolition of zamindary system led to loose the power and authority of the village head. But some religious festivals, such as, rights to worship Bhumsen, the village god, *Khera pujan* are still being done by the village head. No other person of the village has the right to worship, except the village head or the members of the lineage of the village head. At the same time, the village heads are so cooperating and well meaning towards the village members that every one obeys his words and show respect to him. His opinions about the present political affairs are to be given a great weight. And thirdly the traditional Takat, an inter-village panchayat, maintains solidarity and unity of the community through the strict rules of panchayat of the Bhoksa community.

Actually, among the Bhoksa community the traditional elite groups or family members or lineage members are now acting as the present elite groups. The Podhan or Gaon Panchayat heads are the members of the traditional elite groups. Though the Statutory Panchayat are now a new form of the old Panch of the village the only difference is that the old Panch constitutes only with one village, but the Gaon Sabha is constituted with more than one villages. An emerging trend is found that in some of the blocks dominated villages of Panjabs are now the podhans. The present criterio of the elites of the community is treated depending on the behaviour of the persons who have economic status with some education and good contacts with outer agencies. They form a large family with some-what rational orientation to life. The community members or non-community members do not seem to determine leadership. There is a tendency to elect educated persons, who have spare time, good economic condition, honesty, popularity, effective outlook, ability to settle disputes education, organising ability, interest, speaking power, members of families, contact with Govt. officials. These are considered to be the essential qualities of leadership. The emergence of leaders depends mainly upon their individual and personal charms, attraction and other qualities also often weigh in the non-traditional and non-conventional behaviour, but essentially their ability to deliver the goods in crisis is taken into consideration. The informant refered to the fact that even if they succeed in retaining the ledership, the nature of the leadership will change simply because the different castes will now compete with one another for leadership.

The elite constitute a reservior out of which leadership may be drawn and the elites have always the potential for becoming a leader (Chouhan). As mentioned earlier, the endogamous Bhoksa society is segmented into a number of sub-groups and their respective sub-group heads are the traditional elites whose voices carry much weigh. The sub-group heads and also the village heads hold respectable positions in the society. As this society has not maintained any hierarchical stratification, social work or services for their community are the only source of gaining popularity. The support of traditional leaders, i.e., khum-podhan and takat head are some of the significant factors for gaining the superior position of the society.

VIII

From the past, Bhoksas have acquired the reputation of sorcery. In fact, Bhogsar or Bhoksa is the name of a sorcerer in Garhwal. Some are even said to be capable of assuming the form of a wild animal and thus accomplish the destruction of an enemy. Sudarsan? rid Garhwal of sorcerers in the following manner. He called the Bhoksas together under pretence of needing their assistance in some ceremony and promised them all sorts of rewards, should he succeed and so induced them to come with all their books. When all were assembled, they on the pretension of showing power as sorcerers were bound hand and feet and thrown with their books and implements into the river. They have had high reputation for their magic and their skill was believed to work wonders. At present, as they think, there are some Varana in their society who can kill people and call the spirits at their will or make them do many other wonderful things.

Bhoksas say that the magical power of the Bharars has deteriorated with the passage of time, but even today their importance is more or less accepted by them. The magic still protects them from the wild animals save men from snake and scorpion bite, prevents and cures diseases, restores fertility to barren women and foils the mischevious designs of the evil spirits. The Bhoksas believe that the 'mantras' chanted by the Bhararas during many rites and rituals for bringing about definite results have a supernatural sanction behind them and this is responsible for their mystic potency. But the repetition of a mantra is the main thing which imparts efficacy to magic though the mode or pronounciation, communication with the spirits and the physical and mental condition of the Bhararas are the sine-qua-non to bring about the desired effect. The Bhararas must observe fast when they are employed in performing the important rituals, such as, controlling of cholera, etc.

IX

The Bhoksa society is endogamous is nature. They have their community conciousness and community feeling to each other and to members of the community. Marriage or exchange of women with other community is strictly prohibited. They follow partilineal line of inheritance of property and patriarchial type of residence. The elites constitute the reservior out of which leadership may be drawn. An elite has always the potential for becoming a leader (Chouhan). As mentioned earlier, that the endogamous Bhoksa society is segmented into a number of sub-groups and their respective sub-group heads are holding responsible positions in the society. Their personal views are respected by the sub-group members.

X

The traditional Takat Panchayat is very active in its role. In social factors or in some inter-village conflicts the disputes are still being resolved in the Takat Panchayat. But the Takat panchayat and the present Government Statutory Panchayat are working conjointly for maintaining the solidarity of the society and also for getting the benefits of the special measures of Government, for the community through the Statutory Panchayat. The traditional village head or lineage members of the village heads are at present trying to bring a number of Statutory Panchayat. They are most interested in Statutory Panchayats than the traditional Panchayats, because they hold more respectable position than the traditional panchayat. The traditional Panchayat is concerned with the Bhoksa community only. Not only that, the present Statutory Panchayat gives a scope of utilising the government facilities for the benefit of the community and also the officials who are closely associated with them, such as, Ganna society, Panchayat secretary, Serpanch, BDO, ADOm ADC, Cooperative and others show some respect for the suggestions of the podhan of the Gaon Sabha. So, the traditional leaders are now interested in getting elected as members of the Gaon Panchayat or Naya Panchayat. But at present the Bhoksas of Nainital district have organised an organisation in the name of 'Buxas Parishad' at Baria Dawlat of Bazpur Tehsil of Nainital district in 1965-1966 with the aim to social development of the Bhoksa community-philosophical, political, religious and economic. For the above development the Govt. have a plan to set up an organization, library, debating centre, cottage industry, village development centre, development centre in agriculture and a Recreation centre, and it is the duty of the people to help the State and Central Government officials in this regard. The organisation was set up with a managing body of 11 members from among the members of the community.

It is the high caste people who do not evince much interest in the new system of the Panchayat. Since 'Salurmi' is fully dominated by high caste people, the abolition of the 'Salurmi' would mean liquidation of their power. But the low cast people, particularly the Scottas, favour and welcome the new Panchayat. They find that their cases are judged with fariness in the panchayat than Khumri. Moreover, they get better representation in the new Panchayat, while in the Khumri their presence was not required. Now, prior to the decision of cases no *Bistra* (court fee) is required to be paid in the new panchayat system, while in the old one it was essential to deposit this money which varied between Rs. 5/- and Rs. 10/- or more, and sometimes the Panchs were to be entertained with a feast. These are now no longer in practice. As Statutory Gram Panchayat has taken over the functions of the traditional village institutions, the mode of election of members to this new panchayat system, is on the basis of adult franchaise. The traditional leaders' suggestions have no place in the new administrative set up and there is no question of succession to their post. But still the descendants of the old members are honorifically addressed as 'sayanas'. As the post of the podhan is through be election not through the succession.

With regard to the landed property, now all the local people of Jamsar Bawar, irrespective of caste or community, have been distributed land and given ownership right on it. Now there are no zamindar and tenant and in the traditonal Zemindary system. All are at present tenants of the Government. The sale and mortgage of property are nowregistered in the tahsildar's court and 'Sayana' has no function at all. Lands are classified in three categories, according to ownership right-Sibal, Sanjoyute and Land of the forest department. Sibal is owner's own cultivators' land and Sanjoyate is the village community land. Due to the fallow nature of land under the Forest Department, they do not allow for the Mantors.

Conclusion

There are changes in the life of Bhoksas. These changes are due to impact of modernization in one hand, and on the other hands this is due to contact with the other people or outsiders and as a result of these contact changes are perceptible both in material and non material aspects of Bhoksas life. It is evident that contact of the Bhoksas with the others Hindu castes, Muslim, Sikhs and Paharis have brought about fundamental change in material, economic, social and religious sphere of life. But a closer study reveals that the Bhoksas have always been remarkably selective in adoption of alien customs and traits. The Bhoksas have selected or assimilated with suitable adoptions and modifications such elements of alien culture that answered their needs and fitted to their patterns of life and rejected others that were incompatible with their own culture. They have retained their self sufficient economy in some form or the other, mutual reciprocity of obligation. The structure of village community, some of the old traditions and forms connected with birth, marriage and death specially with the religion have been considerably influenced and at the same time they have absorbed a large numbers of elements of more civilized people in their own culture.

In the past, the Bhoksas were in the liberty to change the settlements. They were allotted their choiceable lands by the Khumprodhan in the case of Nainital district, but in the case of Dehradun they had to get aproval from the local Zaminder for the new patches of lands. But due to the Zamindary abolution Act and land revenue Act they become the owner of lands and no further migration is not possible for them as these courage may loose their holding of lands.

So they become settled agriculturist leaving their old habits of shifting cultivations. The present Bhoksas are primarily an agricultural community. Though their agricultural activities are still in subsistance level and the traditonal mode of cultivations procedure is still maintaining its pace. They have the feeling that their agriculture procedure is failed to earn their basic needs through the old methods of agriculture. But due to their unawareness of use of the modern agricultural equipments and procedure for proper rearing agricultural produces to that level do not help this people in agricultural side. So they are keen on improving their agricultural implements and techniques. Thus steel tools and iron implements with better techniques. This involves repairing and further purchases so that these implements by themselves provide sufficient course for sustained contact. By and by, as improved techniques in agriculture have borne fruit in the shape of yield, the marketing of agricultural produce gradually have became a component in their economy. The need for exchange having assorted itself and this is the door through which gradually money economy has been making increasing in roads into the Bhoksas life with its inevitable concomitant of modification of community life. Written bonds and contacts have recently become quite a common features. The co-operative banks is one of the major factors which set up links in money lending process.

In the past all the Bhoksas inhabited villages were uni-ethnic in nature. No other caste groups prefered to live in a settlement along with the Bhoksas, some sporadic cases it was found that some others group make their settlement at the outskirt of the Bhoksa village a near the Bhoksas residence. But at the present it is found that other castes groups of Hindu communities as well as Muslim are living side by side of the Bhoksas, this feature prominently found in the Bhoksas villages of the Dehradun district. Similar trents is also found in the Bhoksas inhabited villages of Nainital district but this is not as prominent as in the Dehradun District. As the living of the Bhoksas in same village is growing, so they have got a scope for the closer interaction among the non-Bhoksas and that influenced the life and culture of the Bhoksas and Bhoksas gradually accepted the some of their (non-Bhoksas) belief. And with that belief of hindu mode of, life is gradually accepting by the Bhoksas *i.e.* Worship of Siva, laxmi, chandi, Ambamali, Hanumanji, Ram & Sita are accepting by the Bhoksas of both the district. The influenced of Hindu deities is found move in the Dehradun district, though Nainital Bhoksas are also accepting the same along with their traditional belief. They visited the worshipping place of Hindu, attend puja and prayed to the God for giving them prosparity as health and gain in the material life. Similarly, they also showed their belief in the Muslims religion a sikhism. They visited Masjid or Gurudwara with a prayer for their material benefit. They also visited Muslim pir or fakir for some treatment when their local Bharara fail to cure the disease of the patient.

The restriction imposed by the forest department, after decleration of the forest as reserved forest. This affected their traditonal occupations of the

Bhoksas such as hunting, collecting of the forest products and building material proved a serious blow to the economic self sufficiency of these people, consequently, resentment is growing among the Bhoksas against of their age old liberties. The relation between Bhoksas and forest officials are worsening every day.

The effect of the indirect rules on the Bhoksas who are governed on the legal code of the country and not by the customary law are not beneficial for the ignorant Bhoksas. Although they still lookforward to their own tribal pancyayat for administering law and justice to them, yet the doors of the civil courts open to them. The judicial official not being conversant with the customs and practices of these people have not been able to impart satisfactory justice to them.

The excise laws makes it illegal to brew rice or mahua beer or any kind of spiritous drink Instead the excise authorities allow the sale of liquor by rapacious merchants at the licensed shops for money price. This situation instead of diminishing the drink habits of the Bhoksas has led to an increase in drunkeness and immorality. Most of the Bhoksas are addicted to drink, even their womenfolk drink and creat a taste for it among the children. Among most of them, liquor is a necessary accompainment of almost all social and religious functions which requires fulfilment of tribal obligations regarding hospitality and entertainment.

Magical practices are appllied to agriculture, disease and other crises relating to birth and marriage ceremonies. Magical methods are also employed in driving away the evil spirits, in warding off the influenced of the evil eye and in curing disease caused by the mother goddess and other supernatural agencies. The educated or concious people are also consulted doctor in the case of ailment and other disease. But the majority still have faith in the Bhoksas Bharara whose magical spells and amulets are believed to be most effective in any crisis of difficulty of the Bhoksas.

The overall effect of a whole concatenation of changes with a more secure and steady source of livelihood in that an incentive to improve their standard of living aline to them has developed specially among the educated people of their community. New wants such as, European dresses, hurrican lanterns, bycycles and cosmetics have appeared in their daily life and they are just tending to be secessaries with the educated and advanced people. Money is required to buy these things and the way of living must also be changed to earn it. Herein lies one of many changes with the attendant change in value of the transition from Money loss economy to a money dominated one. Due to invasion of money economy, the assertion of individual authority and responsibility has been more pronounced in recent years. Consequently neculear family is increasing. As increasing number of people now prefer to cultivate their land independable, sell their own produce spend their income on themselves, their wives and children and live as separate family units. On the other hand, the village community with its co-operatives pattern and strongly knit discipline based on mutual reciprocity of obligations serves to keep alive in the mind of every Bhoksas a feeling of total unity, cohesion and solidarity.

The status of Bhoksas Bharara was among the Bhoksas was too high at an early date. Bhoksas do not start any work without consulting a Bharara. Bharara was their advisor in the case of any misshappening or illness or at any danger of evil eye. Their beliefs in the Bharara and super-natural world is so high that they can got out of it. And at present Bhoksas people become conscious and consulted local doctors or sometimes visited to hospital for some disease. It is also stated that at the present day Bharara themselves advised the local people to consult the doctors if they failed to cure any patients by their local treatment.

The common practice with the liquor seller who are outsiders mostly is to exploit the innocents and simplicity of Bhoksas by selling liquor to them on credit and the charge exorbetant rate of interest which goes on accumulating to enormous amounts in course of a few years. Many Bhoksas have been totally ruined on account of drinking habit and exploitation of liquire sellers.

The unregulated and ill planned reform movements with their insistance upon the abandonment of old customs and practices, rites and ritual under the pressure of the Hindu caontanct have brought the Bhoksas many changes to them.

a) By inviting Brahmin in various ceremonies such as birth, marriage and death, the Bhoksas have to incurred a lot of money for expenditure.

b) Contact has also brought less desirable customs of the Hindus caste system such as dietary restriction have increased.

c) The restriction on the freedom of their women folk have created an agitation among the women themselves who have defied at times such a ban on their age old liberty. This situation has created a lot of trouble in the Bhoksas community as men do not have much controll over their women. The result has been that happiness of family life has been broken down in many case and bickerings have increased.

Education as such have no encouraging impact on the community in general. On the literacy front, performance of fair sex is quite shocking. But it is not wrong to say that modern education is slowly spreading among them. Due to their continuous contact with the other caste people the Bhoksas are now interested in education of their children.

References

1. Government of India : 1961 : Census of India Vol.-I. Monograph Series, Part V-B (IV).

BUKSA

A Scheduled Tribe in Uttar Pradesh.

Office of the Registrar General New Delhi

2. Government of India : 1971 : Census of India.

3. Crook, W. : 1896 : The tribes and castes of North Western Provinces and Oudh. Vol.-II.

4. Turner, A.C. : 1931 : Census Report of United Provinces.

5. Atkinson, E.T. : 1886 : The Himalayan Districts of North Western Provinces of India Vol.I.

6. Atkinson, E.T. : 1886 : The Himalayan District of North Western Provinces of India-Vol.III.

7. Rizvi, S.M.H. : 1976 : Some Aspect of physical growth among Bhoksa boys.

& Tandon, V.K. Research Bulletin, Department of Anthropology, Lucknow University, Lucknow, India.

INDEX

T

T

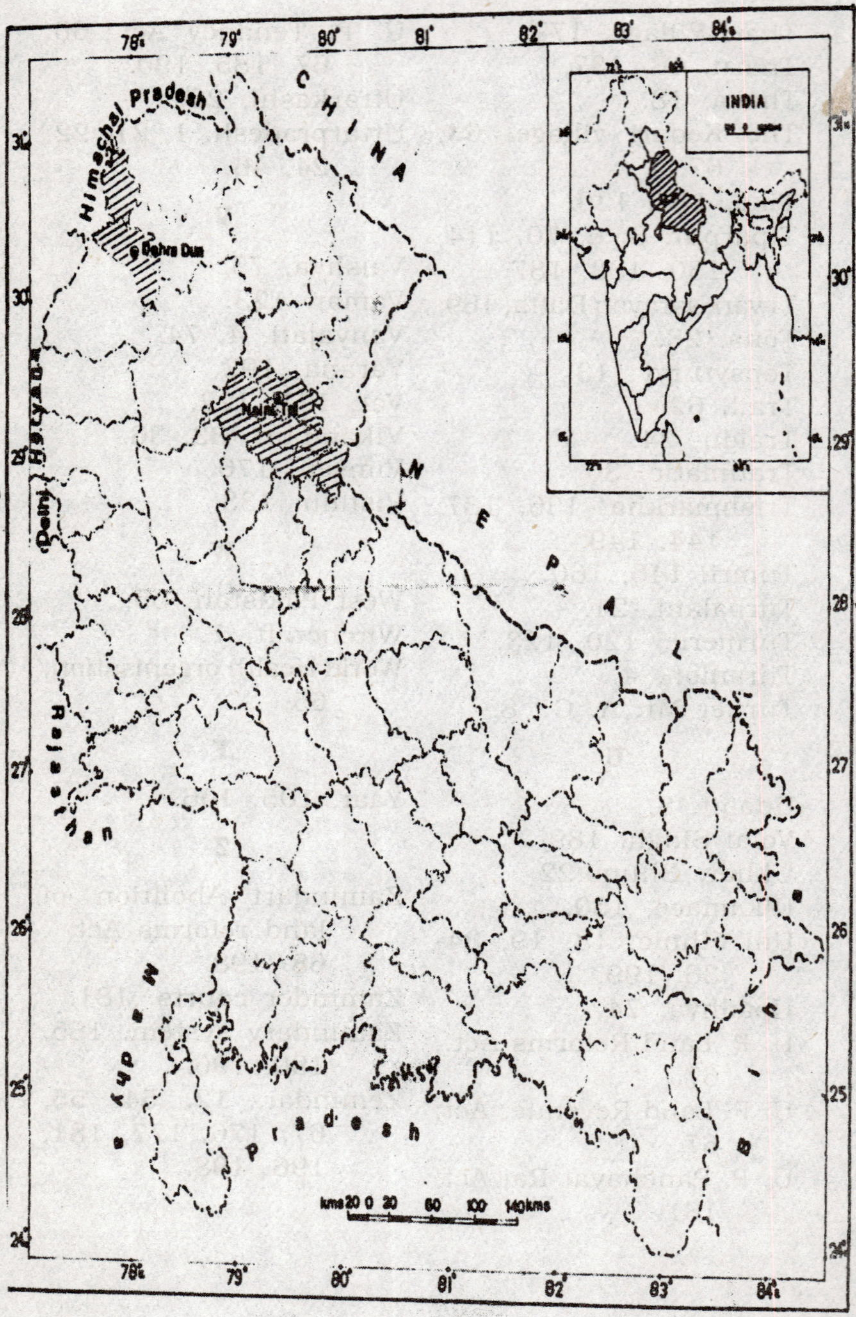
CHINA
NEPAL
Himachal Pradesh
Haryana
Delhi
Rajasthan
Madhya Pradesh
Bihar
Dehra Dun
Naini Tal
INDIA
kms 20 0 20 60 100 140 kms
78°
79°
80°
81°
82°
83°
84°
31°
30°
29°
28°
27°
26°
25°
24°

PLATE-I (A)

Bhoksa Man

Tiparpur, Dheradun

PLATE-I (B)

Place of Forest God Saiad

Tiparpur, Dheradun

PLATE-II (C)

Woman Personal Care
Pipalsanna, Nainital

PLATE-(2) D

Sericulture Work
Tiparpur, Dehradun

PLATE-(III)E

Bhoksa Woman Pulling Drinking Water
Tiparpur, Dehradun

PLATE-(III)F

Profile of Bhoksa Woman
Khum Bari, Nainital

PLATE-(IV) G

Bhoksa Woman working after the household works
Tiparpur, Dehradun

PLATE-(IV) H

Bhoksa working as Badai
Pipalsanna, Nainital

PLATE-(V) I

Bhoksa preparing erectrical Item in house
Pipalsanna, Nainital

PLATE-(V) J

A Khum Podhan
Pipalsanna, Nainital

PLATE-(VI) K

Bhoksa Woman with Chilam
Pipalsanna, Nainital

PLATE-(VI) L

Bhoksa Preparing Traditional Charpai
Pipalsanna, Nainital

PLATE-(VII) M

Balbadi School
Medinipur & Bodipur, Dehradun

PLATE-(VII) N

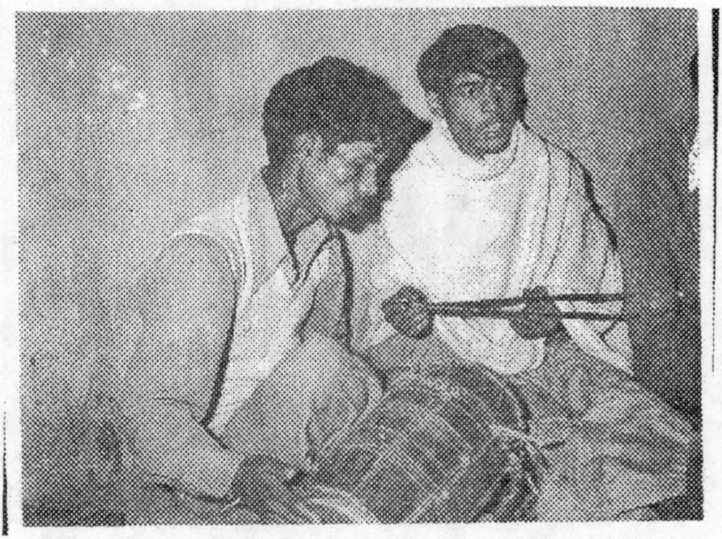

Singing Song Praising God & Goddesses
Tiparpur, Dehradun

PLATE-(VIII) O

Bhoksa Mother with Child
Pipalsanna, Nainital

PLATE-(VIII) P

Husking grain
Pipalsanna, Nainital

PLATE-(VII) M

Balbadi School
Medinipur & Bodipur, Dehradun

PLATE-(VII) N

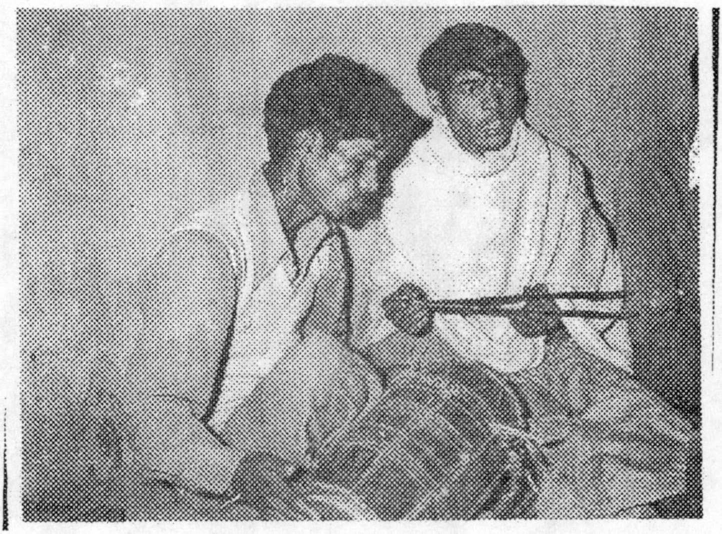

Singing Song Praising God & Goddesses
Tiparpur, Dehradun

PLATE-(VIII) O

Bhoksa Mother with Child
Pipalsanna, Nainital

PLATE-(VIII) P

Husking grain
Pipalsanna, Nainital

PLATE-(XI) Q

Bhoksa looking after the household goods
Tiparpur, Dehradun

PLATE- (IX) R

Bhoksa woman of the Ages
Pipalsanna, Nainital

PLATE- (X) S

Bhoksa women Handicrafts
Khumbari, Nainital

PLATE- (X) T

Bhoksa Carpentar
Tiparpur, Dehradun

PLATE-(XI) Q

Bhoksa looking after the household goods
Tiparpur, Dehradun

PLATE- (IX) R

Bhoksa woman of the Ages
Pipalsanna, Nainital

PLATE- (X) S

Bhoksa women Handicrafts
Khumbari, Nainital

PLATE- (X) T

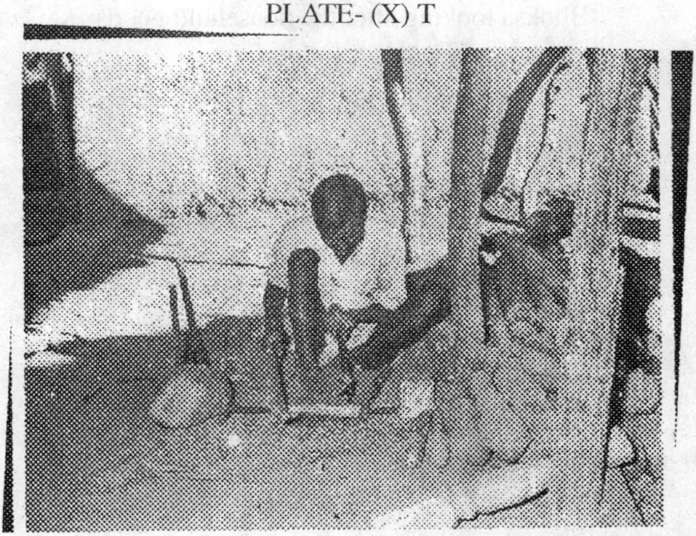

Bhoksa Carpentar
Tiparpur, Dehradun

PLATE-(XI) U

A Bhoksa Young Girl
Pipalsanna, Nainital

PLATE-(XI) V

Women Participating Making Rope
Tiparpur, Dehradun

PLATE-(XII) W

A Bhoksa Couple
Tiparpur, Dehradun